I0467563

Lobotomy

The Marginalisation of Creativity and How to Become Human Again

Mike Fitzsimons (MBA)   Sue Bradley (MA)

Dedications

Mike
For Kate and Michael, the future is yours

Sue
For Tim, my mum Joyce and my beloved house rabbits
Bunsen and Scuttley

Copyright © 2016 Mike Fitzsimons and Sue Bradley
All rights reserved.
ISBN-13: 978-1530077144

Acknowledgements

We would like to thank the following for their help, advice and input over the six years that this book has taken to write. Richard Sant from The University of Portsmouth who gave much of his valuable time to help us formulate a research approach to test our theories and questions and who challenged us on many ideas that otherwise would have made this book an unending task. All the staff at Creative Partnerships Southampton and Isle of Wight who provided input and feedback perhaps sometimes unknowingly, but who helped us to understand the bigger picture: Erica Smith, Jane Bryant, Janet Aughey, Joe Ross, Liz Kent, Sally Beattie, Naomi Lahiff, Andrew Snow, Stephen Boyce, and many others who worked in and around the project. Sue Lawther for providing interview material, reviewing our early draft and helping to guide our thoughts and ideas. Roy Hutchins for providing candid interviews and honest feedback. Paul Levy who read and re-read our draft manuscript provoking us in his good natured but unerring way to make many essential improvements. Our life partners Tim Pilcher and Liz Fitzsimons for supporting us throughout this journey and for also suggesting many additions and changes that have strengthened our book. The greatest thanks must go to Mary Matthews, our final editor and literacy advisor. Despite retiring some years ago from editorship roles with the Oxford University Press and The Londoner (The former Greater London Council (GLC) newspaper) she took on the task of turning our prose into a readable and consistent book.

We must also add Wikipedia and Google without which our research would have been almost impossible to complete in the limited time that was available in both our lives.

Illustration

Cover illustration by Lauren Crow
E: info@laurencrow.co.uk
www.laurencrow.co.uk

Back Cover Portrait of Sue Bradley by Sophie Sheinwald
E: sophie@sophiesheinwald.com
www.sophiesheinwald.com

Contents

Appendix

Creativity takes courage

Henri Matisse

About the authors

Mike Fitzsimons

Mike graduated from Essex University in 1972, and pursued a career in music until taking a job in social research in 1975. He quickly entered the fast-growing computer sector specialising in data analysis and in 1985 headed the BBC's IT section of the audience research team. He has given numerous talks on prediction techniques to international audiences. Mike has also played with several UK bands, the most notable being The Piranhas (top 10 single) and The Papers (Top 5 indie single) and was signed to EMI and Radioactive Records. Currently he has a music publishing deal in Nashville and owns his own song writing and music production company. He became fascinated by the relationship between creativity and business after working with Sue as a consultant on a programme designed to raise standards in education by using creative methods of teaching and learning.

Qualifications:
MBA Innovation and Business
BA (Hons) Economics

About the authors

Sue Bradley

Sue worked as a musician and performer in the 1980s with bands and physical theatre companies such as Pookiesnackenburger and Ra Ra Zoo, touring internationally. She was a scriptwriter and actor for London Weekend Television, co-wrote and acted in her own Channel 4 TV series and was signed to Stiff records with her band. Throughout the 1990s she was Head of Expressive Arts in a large urban secondary school. In 2001 she became Creative Director for England's flagship creative education programme, Creative Partnerships, managed by Arts Council, England. More recently she has been a marketing executive for a TV station. Currently she manages her own business as a yoga teacher and food educator, helping people to redefine their relationship with food via a bespoke change management programme

Sue gave a TEDx talk on this book's topic in 2011 to an audience of academics, journalists and the general public and has significant media experience.

Qualifications:
MA (Ed) Multiple Intelligences and Learning Styles
PG Dip Drama Education
PGCE Secondary Education (Music)
BA (Hons) 11.1 Visual and Performing Arts
RYT500 Yoga Teacher
Certified Eating Psychology Coach (IPE)

Preface: How did we get here?

This is a book about how our world has become unnaturally divided. Our human capabilities have been railroaded into one of two camps, the logical or the creative, and each have been assigned different values, leading to a damaging conflict that undermines our future.

But before we begin, we would like to introduce ourselves and tell you a bit about the journey we have each taken to reach this point and how our book 'Lobotomy' came about.

Mike

I was walking down Bexleyheath High Street, a run-down suburb of South London, looking for the shop, late on December 24th 1962, and I wished I'd worn my gloves. My dad next to me, setting a fast pace, my twin brother on his other side, a year of our savings in his pockets - £10. A low drumming sound getting louder, then an escaping note or two as the shop door opened and closed, much older boys hanging around smoking, drinking beer, long hair, thin jeans, girls. We stood at the window, eyes locked on the instruments, faces lit by the flashing neon. Guitars of all colours hung from the walls, amplifiers stacked up on the floor, drum kits sat sparkling at the back. 'Which one d'ya want'. Strong working hands rested on our shoulders. We gazed at the models neither of us could play yet. One pick-up red and black - £19, two pick-ups white - £25, three pick -ups blue and cream - £35. My dad had said he'd match what we'd saved. For two 11-year olds doing paper rounds and odd jobs for a year in 1962, £10 was pretty good going. Two pick-ups were essential and the minimum, as no-one good played a single pick-up guitar. He pulled out a roll of bills, licked his thumb, peeled off £15, 'there y'are' now go ahead and buy yer guitar'. It would be another year until we could afford the amplifier.

Sue

Sitting on the village bench in hot-pants with my best friend, also called Sue, we collected wolf whistles from young male drivers of passing cars. The two Sues tallying totals over an hour, even two. Village life was very dull. I would say comfortable, but I had never known real material discomfort, so I took it for granted and felt typical teenage angst. I rode my pushbike past our newly built, 1960s detached house, one of a row, each with its own neat lawn. Life was punctuated with interminably dull family caravan holidays, piles of library books, a transistor radio with an earpiece, girl guides, mending clothes, and good, plain, traditional English food. I read about what seemed like rumours of the existence of another kind of life, where you weren't expected to have a brief career, then marry a nice respectable boy with a good job (or maybe, in my case, a businessman who was also my boss), and have 2.4 children. Out there was a world where you could apparently play in a band, go to parties and hang out on street corners, and live in something called a 'shared house'. I didn't even know about theatres and I yearned to go to a gig.

Mike

Our new school was brutal. Built for those who failed their 11+ test, a 1950s secondary modern, boys, Roman Catholic, based in South London, run by a menacing order of religious brothers, whose aim was to produce tough working men. Electric guitars had no place in this school. A few of us persevered - music had become 'youth culture' - and it was now unavoidable. Lennon, McCartney, Harrison and Starr ably abetted by Jagger and Richards had seen to that. Getting a force 10 caning across the hands was a regular occurrence. No one was allowed to blub though, the consequences of that were worse, your classmates would tear you to shreds forever. No forgiveness, no excuses, there was no escape. I still come across insane people who think this was good idea. Perhaps it never happened to them. But somehow the music prevailed, and the guitar brought a coolness to my life that kept the bullying crowd away. I developed a thirst for knowledge of all kinds that became the beat I wanted to follow. The school improved, a band was formed and things were looking up. I worked on building sites at weekends with my dad, we drank beer in pubs, I studied, and I played. Bagging the right number of A levels for university got me and my twin brother out of the South London suburbs for ever. My motivations were complex and diverse, I never wanted to be short of money again; I didn't want to live in fear, with no aspirations other than to work at the local factory; I wanted to be free of the religious shackles; I wanted to learn; and I wanted to play music. I was going to break out; I was intelligent, young and full of ideas.

Sue

School was a disappointment. It was the year of the secondary modern and grammar schools merger into the new comprehensive system. Considered a 'swot' by my peers, I sat reading books under the table in English class, whilst paper planes and insults flew through the air above me. I was one of only about a dozen pupils taking O-levels rather than CSEs, as academic success was the only way out of the village that I knew of. This led to bullying, compounded by the fact that I played the violin. Not good.

Mike

Leaving university behind in 1972, bumming around in building jobs for a year, trying to succeed as a bass player in a semi-pro jazz-rock band, a new reality began to nag at me. I was poor, and the prospects of being a successful musician were remote. I wanted something more than this. I wanted a job and a career. I wanted to use my shiny new degree as a ticket to somewhere better. I had three guitars, all the amplification I'd ever need, I could play, I had girl friends, but for me this road was leading nowhere. Gigs were becoming a drag, the band argued all the time, they threw away chance after chance on some trumped-up musical principle or claim that it would undermine their unique talent. I was shackled to a dead weight.

I eventually found long-term stable employment working as a researcher in a fledgling government department, dealing in high value, dangerous statistics. That is: information you could use to convince the money men that you needed more cash to plan and build the next hospital, school, road, airport, or sports stadium. It's true that music had inspired me, but this was something new, this was me 'making it'. From here on music started to take a back seat.

The office was full of enthusiastic, intelligent, radical, idealistic, savvy young people from all walks of life with a high proportion of heavenly females, including my boss. Located near London's Covent Garden: pubs, restaurants and theatres, the West End and the river Thames, I doubt anyone could have been happier. The office was hip and friendly. Problems dripped from every wall, people wrestling with new concepts, ideas, working late, arguments, celebrations - it had a buzz you could eat.

I'd previously had a few months' experience of office life in a merchant bank where every desk had a 'bloke' in a blue suit chained to it, and a secretarial pool of mini-skirted typists. It was a 'bloke' culture that meant you drank at lunchtime, tried your luck with the typists in the afternoon, and bellowed instructions at staff if you wanted something done. Added to this were a clutch of student summer jobs in rabid offices with equally perverse cultures and behaviours, some that I found largely indigestible and even sickening. But I had learned along the way. Photocopying, filing, form- filling, desks, timekeeping, management, duties, meetings, lunch, commuting, teams, promotion, suits, rules, bonuses, overtime, salary - they were all familiar to me.

Sue

I dropped out of Art College at the beginning of the third year to hit the road. I had so many gigs lined up with my electric violin and band, and so many parties to go to and countries to visit and theatre companies and circuses to join, there was no time to stay in one place. I was flying.

As a performer, I wore what people who were performers wore – which generally consisted of stuff that nobody else wore. Lots of what would now be termed 'vintage', but at the time just meant it was from charity shops or hand-me-downs, mixed with a bit of punk stuff and circusy type imagery, such as stripy tights and gypsy-style scarves. I never sported labels or brands, and my look was colourful and individual. I was once asked to pose for a photo with an American tourist, who asked what my mother thought about how I looked. I had on a Victorian pink polka dot nightie, belted, with shiny pink lycra dancers' tights (as worn by UK female rock band 'The Slits'), a pink 1960s woollen coat, which had been my mother's, and spiky self-cut hair, bleached then coloured with magenta crazy colour. I wasn't sure what my mother thought, but I remember my father informing me that the punk make-up I was wearing didn't make me look at all attractive. I was, of course, pleased by this – for me, it was applied to create a particular effect. Once, when I was still living at home with my parents, I was banned from the local pub on the grounds that I had 'deliberately made myself look stupid'. To make a point I went home and put on a pale green knitted viscose skirt suit belonging to my mother, together with beige tights and soft make up. They said I looked even more stupid.

Twelve years of international touring later, as I lay in my hammock on the island where South Pacific was filmed, idly watching monkeys wave stolen pairs of sunglasses from palm trees at travellers whose patience was wearing thin, I guiltily reflected on the fact that I was shortly about to give up on a life that many people would regard as their own personal utopia. America, Australia, Hong Kong all blurred into one big whirl of sex, drugs and rock and roll, of making new friends in bars only to leave them, dazed and confused. Always moving on, with pockets and bags weighed down with donated copper and silver, and intellectual boredom dulled by endless pints of free lager. It was hard to say goodbye to that lifestyle. My very core being, my identity, was wrapped up in this way of life. When I returned to my home town, Brighton in the UK, who would I be without a wealth of fascinating and constantly replenished traveller's tales to tell? What would I have to talk about? Who was I, in fact? This is what I needed to know. What did I prefer: going out or staying in? And if going out, to do what? I couldn't imagine ever wanting to pay for entertainment such as gigs or shows. That was my way of life. Also holidays –why would I ever want to take one of those? My life was just one long holiday.

I once went to see an accountant, who was trying to explain that most people make money to fund the activities they take part in when not working. In my life, it could be said that the term 'business expense' could be applied either to every single thing I did or bought, or conversely nothing that I did or bought, as I had no concept of how to separate the two. After a gig in Singapore I had a week of no work before the next gig in Norway. The cheapest place to hang out for the week was Malaysia. Was that a holiday? The accountant asked. No, I said, mystified; it was just the cheapest place to live. He sighed and decided I was running some kind of scam.

Mike

My new employer had the world's biggest problem - computers. They had no-one to program them. I'd done a short course at university and a lot of econometric computer modelling on a 'PDP 10', so I dutifully volunteered. Just 50% of my time - just to help out. I was consumed by the machines for evermore. At that time a machine the size of a house could add up a large series of numbers pretty quickly and reasonably accurately, surrounded by men in white coats, cooled by water in a sealed air- conditioned room; very useful in the financial sector and becoming essential in the world of statistics. By the time the machines grew tired of me over 30 years later, a more powerful machine was in my pocket waiting for my phone calls and text messages, helping me run my life, plugging me into the new 'digital world'.

Sue

When I first entered the teaching profession it was as a student teacher, although I was already in my thirties by that time. I always made it very clear to the pupils that I was 'not really a teacher'. No, I was a performer, who happened to be doing a bit of teaching, that's all. I still wore my sturdy seamed dance tights and boots, although now with what I would term as 'normal' skirts and tops. When I started my first job I made a real effort to pass as normal. I went to Wallis, a mainstream women's clothing shop, and bought an entire outfit. When I wore it to school the next day my tutor group said I still looked weird. They couldn't quite put their finger on why, but I did. After a while they got used me and I once received a standing ovation for a particularly outrageous pair of shoes. But as the years wore on I learned that the clothes were a distraction and what the kids really wanted and respected was a quite dull and boring look. Conservative with a small c. So eventually, I morphed into my environment and began to look like everyone else. I had no idea what I really liked any more - I thought I was becoming too old to carry off the punky street performer look without looking like a bag lady - but I knew I didn't like the straight teacher look either. I had been playing the role of teacher for so long, I could no longer remember who I was - or rather, I was completely out of touch with whoever or whatever I had become. I only saw myself reflected through the eyes of a thousand teenagers.

For my final MA project I designed a series of lessons, each based around a different type of learning style or 'intelligence' such as visual, musical or 'learning by doing'. Theoretically, we each have a preferred way of learning, and the likelihood is that teachers deliver lessons according to what worked for them as pupils. Many teachers are 'reading and writing' learners and it doesn't occur to them that this way of learning might not suit everybody. As I was teaching drama and music, I assumed that I must have a very hands on approach, which would be good for all types of learner. However, when I came to teach a drama lesson in a way that suited kids who had the type of brain that liked maths, I suddenly found that lots of children, who up until then had not liked drama, suddenly became stars for the day, and it was because of how I was presenting the material.

This led to a whole new way of teaching for me. The more I was able to understand how different people learn, the more I loosened up. I remember one lesson where some boys had finished their work before anyone else. When I praised them they were so pleased that, before I could stop them, they had jumped out of the seats and were running around the edge of the classroom in some kind of 'Victory lap'. Instead of defining this as bad behaviour, I realised that it was just what that type of kid needed to do, so I constructed a furniture-free circuit around the edges of the room. I made sure every lesson contained 'ways in' for all types of learner.

Mike

For me the office provided parties, hangovers, humour, love, friends, holidays, money, status, security, learning, challenges, and opportunities in every direction. The hierarchy worked. The longer I stayed the more I understood. The chances of promotion came, I moved up and I started managing the new learners. The mumblings of huddled senior managers behind closed doors, which seemed to have no obvious value, started to add up. They weren't discussing me or my world, a world of today, or tomorrow, or even next week. On their minds was next year, or the next five - using what information they had to make snap decisions that they might get hung out to dry for if they screwed up, or maybe promoted for if they didn't. Bang goes job, house, life - maybe for all of us. That didn't mean they were any good at this. They had been promoted through the organisation, and now this was their lot, guessing games in a casino with no cocktails, music or love, slugging it out in a broken-down gym with a bored audience and a sleeping referee.

Sue

I wasn't sure if I remembered Stoney or not. I had been teaching for 12 years, up to five classes a day, 30 pupils in each class, all different. Each class had drama once a fortnight and I taught the whole of years 7-9, plus my GCSE classes, so I saw over 600 children a week. I was supposed to know all their names, have a knowledge of their special needs (around a quarter to a third of pupils in each class would have some kind of individual education plan bringing issues ranging from anger management to anxiety, from cerebral palsy to those on Ritalin for ADHD) and be able to produce a report on their progress at the end of each term.

I did remember Stoney, although not his name at first. He had been caught stealing on many occasions and was difficult, but not violent, in class. Now here he was, at Brighton station asking for change, in a tired and emotional state. 'Ooh look at you, all grown up and handsome'. I flattered him to avoid any potential nasty scenes, as he enveloped me in another unsteady hug. His life story and undying affection for me began to pour out. I felt unworthy. How many kids had passed through my life, and how many had I not been able to help due to the demands of the job and sheer volume of pupils to be assessed and reported on. I was exhausted and felt inhuman.

In the world of a mainstream secondary school, no-one has the time or the emotional energy to look after themselves, let alone anyone else. I suddenly realised how emotionally impoverished my life had become, how I was failing these children who desperately needed someone to talk to at school at break or lunchtime, but how at these times I was always either taking a drama club or on duty. It was non-stop. Then I remembered looking at more senior members of staff when I first became a teacher and vowing that if ever I started to look washed out and hollow in the way that some of them did, it would be time to go. I thought about how I felt and realised that the time had come.

Mike

The office came with a lot of baggage: dress codes, rules, behaviours, clocking in and out and a network of people. By the time I'd moved on to a new employer and taken up a more senior job, I knew hundreds of people I could contact on any one day. To keep all this working, the rules meant everyone obeyed protocol, stuff got done in order, people you would never have over for dinner would work alongside you and leave their overt social preferences at the door. This artificial environment was necessary. The more I moved with the beat the more this life began to dominate. Seduced by the power, status and seemingly unsolvable endless puzzles soon my real life, the one containing my partner, children, friends, family and music, was getting infected. I needed a way out.

Sue

Although I had no intention of joining the senior management of my school, as head of the drama department I had been taking a module called 'Leading from the Middle'. This introduced me to theories of management and leadership for the first time ever, and to my surprise I found it very interesting. The people who came to train us talked about things I had never heard of such as SMART targets - I suddenly found myself feeling less marginalised and more able to assume a position of confidence. Whilst taking this course I remember sitting looking at the job advertised in the paper I had picked up in the staffroom. It was calling for several people to head up teams to run a new Creative Education initiative called Creative Partnerships (CP). The advert had cited a publication called 'All our Futures'. I read it and was amazed to finally find something in education that was inspirational. So I applied to CP. I called in all the help that I could to complete the very long and involved application form, to help me to redefine my experiences into something that would make sense. Two of the people who helped me were my band member Mike, and his wife Liz.

Mike

I'd got used to management speak. It's a bridge. I enjoyed expressing and consuming information in a language that gave me authority to say what I thought, and gave me weapons to fight with: data, analysis, outcomes and so on. I enjoyed dealing with others who couldn't or wouldn't get it, and I enjoyed talking to those who did. It was an endlessly complex, beautiful and obscure language of money, success, boardrooms, smart elegant people, expense accounts, a house in the country and swimming pools. Then there was plain speaking, for the troops or the old guard, simply telling it like it is - which was nonsense, and usually led to an impasse followed by anger, back-stabbings, swearing etc. The odd curse, just to show you were human after all, worked well.

Sue

At CP I decided to try and play the part straight away. I had heard that Debenhams did a personal shopper service free of charge. So I phoned them up and issued the instruction 'I want to find clothes that turn me from a dull-looking teacher into an arty, perhaps slightly quirky, but well-dressed professional'.

I came away with armfuls of my new image. A smart navy blue Jasper Conran suit, with both trousers and a mid-length, slightly fishtailed skirt, and matching pointy navy court shoes. Tops made from shiny acrylic material with square and sweetheart necklines. Two trouser suits with ruffled blouses, and a navy and white patterned dress with cream wool jacket and a bright red 'seal the deal' shirt. I was dressed for success.

Mike

Applying the corporate mindset to my music career didn't work. I had tried a few times, but no-one wanted to know. You get treated like a 'suit', a disparaging term used by musicians about anyone who deals with money. Return on investment is not a phrase you'll hear on the streets of the music biz. Stuff like career planning or aims and objectives will consign you to the stocks. I even tried to set up a music related business in 1999, to gather data from the fledgling music websites, to create the 'download chart'. We were advised that it would never happen, and no one would ever invest is such a concept. Sue, on the other hand, was beginning to struggle with all this 'suit' language. As a director she now had to deal with it. Now there were stakeholders, politicians to please and sceptics to convince, money to be managed and accounted for, staff to deal with, advocacy to be developed. Ammunition would be needed, so inevitably we started to talk.

Sue

A few weeks later I was sitting on a high-speed ferry feeling quite the smart professional about town. The stylish dress and cream wool jacket were drawing admiring glances from the sort of man who had never glanced admiringly at me before, which I found oddly embarrassing. I had to pick my way along paths and pavements in my kitten heels, having been used to striding along in chunky boots. This was definitely a much better person to be. Yes. In charge of my own time, free to sit and have a coffee and send an email from my new-fangled Blackberry whenever I wanted to. Life was very good indeed!

Mike

I reached 55 without a heart attack or a by-pass, with some serious business qualifications and a trunkful of experience, the baggage of a government and private sector corporate career, and then retired. This was always my plan, five years late, but it worked out. My partner and my kids were ecstatic. I had been developing into a corporate bore, now I could dump all that. My other career in music could restart. Not serious music. No exams, no qualifications, just freedom to be creative and do what I loved doing. The two didn't intersect. Or so I thought.

Somewhere along this road, I met Sue, the fiddle player in The Blue Hearts, a band I started playing with over 20 years ago. Strangely, despite the many years we've played music together, we knew very little about each other. Music was our crossing point.

It all began when Sue asked for advice about the job application. Liz, my partner, has a keen eye and real talent for CV production and sorting out career directions. So she advised Sue on her CV. When Sue got the job, I was intrigued by her new role. The big idea, about creative learning, seemed to make good sense. Our kids, Michael and Kate were still going through traditional education, and they were experiencing a mixed bag of learning trickery - some good, some bad. Not only that, but their peer group - a wide, diverse crowd of sharp, bright kids - were getting the same formal diet, with mixed results.

I wanted to keep my corporate career ticking along, earning some consultancy crust, but keeping it as a hobby rather than a day job. So I thought I might be a useful hand to help with setting up the programme. Sue agreed.

And that's it. What happened next was warfare. Not angry warfare, but a realisation that we had discovered two opposing worlds, when we both thought we were living in one.

You won't hear any more about us as individuals, but you will hear our individual voices throughout this book, as we work out why sometimes we simply cannot understand one another...

Part 1: Discovery and tests

Part 1: Chapter 1: Overview of the Lobotomy

'The intuitive mind is a sacred gift and the rational mind is a faithful servant. We have created a society that honours the servant and has forgotten the gift.'

— Albert Einstein

Are you happy? Do you ever wake up and feel your life is dull, or perhaps you constantly worry about making enough money to live on? Is your work satisfying, or does it leave you drained and empty? If you have children, do you worry about their future, imprisoned by technology and lacking any spark of individuality? Do you see jobs vanishing, industries crumbling? Are you aware of the many global problems that seem to lack any viable solutions? Does your city look like it has lost its heart, with empty high streets and out-of - town shopping malls? Then it sounds like you are being affected by a cultural 'lobotomy', a term we use to describe a process that encourages us to become either logical or creative but not both. Either our creative abilities are subjugated by a world of tasks that require us to be constantly rational and logical, or our logical abilities are dismissed as evil by a creative fashion that abhors organisation and wealth. The roots of this malaise can be found within industrialisation, then accelerated by mass production and the development of the assembly line: a process that requires folk to do simple things all day long. Mass production depends on and values the logical and managerial, as opposed to the creative and emotional capabilities of our brain. As a consequence two subcultures have emerged: one promoting our logical organisational skills, the other championing our creative abilities. Unfortunately these two world views have become opponents slugging it out in academic, political, and economic battlegrounds. This is having a negative impact on our experience of life and threatens our future. We live in a rapidly dividing world. It is as if someone has lobotomised humans; torn apart the connections that link creativity and logic, stating that from now on we can be one or the other, but not both. But it's really just a façade. It is reversible, it is curable, and it is possible to get back in touch with our complete selves. Of course, if you've been working in a corporate environment all your life it's going to be tougher to restart those connections than if you are a three-year-old who hasn't been to school yet. If you're an artist who can't make ends meet, it may take some time to get the connections to your logical self started up and business acumen developed in order to sustain you, but they are there, waiting to be used. You can make your business more successful, your enterprises more relevant and your personal life more fulfilling. Read on to get your life back on track, make business more profitable, and build a more sustainable future. The lobotomy can be eradicated.

If the lobotomy is such a threat, has it emerged in previous civilisations and been responsible for their demise? Depending whose point of view you take, previous civilisations have collapsed for reasons of war, exhaustion of resources, catastrophe, population depletion, over-population, corruption, disease, conquests and fear. The reasons are in many cases supported by historical evidence, but must necessarily include some conjecture and subjective interpretation of the facts. Finding the common conditions of failure for all civilisations is a pastime of guesstimates, estimates and painstaking research. The West, which is our contemporary civilisation, and by many measures the most successful to date, has provided the most effective system of creative endeavour ever developed, a system that has allowed ideas to flow and has encouraged its citizens to think freely, unhampered by birth, religion, gender, age or race. No one before the 20th century had stood on the moon, no one had found a cure for tuberculosis or could prevent malaria. No one championed the rights of women and no machine could send a message instantly around the world to millions of people. In contrast slavery was a hallmark of the past, as was endless war and a short life. In the West imperfections exist, but in history whether we explore China before the 17th century or Roman or Greek civilisations, human freedom to think creatively was tempered by draconian rules, rigid class hierarchies and brutal punishments, often reinforced by a conservative religious politic.

Our question then is: is our civilisation, the West, at risk? The ingredients that gave rise to the West can be stirred and cooked in many ways in an attempt to find the winning formula, but one thing is clear. The unbridled combination of creativity and logic was fundamental. Whether it manifests in the division of labour as technology, architecture, farming, music or law, it has at its root the power of humanity to bring together these two abilities to build a durable successful future and solve the most intractable of problems. Our view is that we are corrupting this vital universe, undoing one of the primary principles of our civilisation, and once again giving succour to elites that have little interest in maintaining something they do not value.

This book describes how the links between our creative and our logical capabilities are being severed to satisfy the machine of corporate culture whilst creativity is deified as the preserve of elitist artistic martyrs and puritans. Our creativity is being relentlessly devalued to make way for more 'rational' consumption, unwavering obedience and less independent thought. At the same time creativity is being sidelined into an arts activity, surrounded by pompous elitisms divorced from the world of work and logic. And yet the solution is simple: reconnect our creativity and logic.

About 250 years ago, the industrial revolution began in the West and changed the world forever. Mass production and cheap consumer goods have become the norm. Whilst this has delivered fabulous wealth and well-being for many of us, it has also introduced new working methods that began to divide our minds and reward our logical selves for compliance. Medical science attempted to mimic this new zeitgeist by developing theories of brain lateralisation. This proposed that the two hemispheres of the brain were indeed separate, and 'managed' different parts of human activity, namely the creative imaginative right side v the logical left. Although this theory is now discredited the battle lines were drawn up and remain to this day.

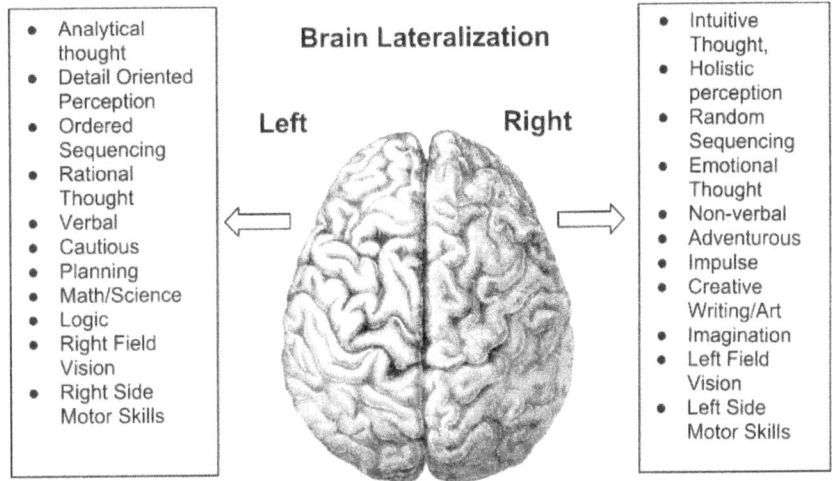

Brain Lateralization

Left   **Right**

- Analytical thought
- Detail Oriented Perception
- Ordered Sequencing
- Rational Thought
- Verbal
- Cautious
- Planning
- Math/Science
- Logic
- Right Field Vision
- Right Side Motor Skills

- Intuitive Thought,
- Holistic perception
- Random Sequencing
- Emotional Thought
- Non-verbal
- Adventurous
- Impulse
- Creative Writing/Art
- Imagination
- Left Field Vision
- Left Side Motor Skills

http://en.wikipedia.org/wiki/File:Brain_Lateralization.svg

The inspiration for this book began when we noticed how people we'd worked with on arts and business projects seemed to have an irrational antipathy towards each other; they behaved as if they lived by a different set of values, almost as if they inhabited opposite sides of a canyon - a yawning gap defined by being either creative or business minded. Colleagues of the same age group, equally intelligent, qualified and socially aware, displayed an ingrained contempt for the other side. There is no denying that this divide exists. Why it does is the story of this book. The stereotypes are there for us to see, writ large in the media, the abuse traded subtly through language, life styles, dress codes and attitudes. For example, in the arts and entertainment fields paying customers are often referred to disparagingly as 'punters'; anyone who deals with organisation or money is referred to as a 'suit', a deliberate insult aimed to paint them as mindless drones. Similarly, creatives are ostracised, sensationalised, accused of being unworldly and lazy, using recreational drugs and relying on hand-outs. What we saw and experienced looked and felt like social prejudice, coupled with a form of defensive arrogance emanating from both sides.

On the surface, having an arrogant attitude towards another group may seem innocuous and of no consequence. However as we will see, in this case it's having a very damaging impact on our future well-being. We believe we have reached a tipping point. If these attitudes are allowed to continue we will find it increasingly difficult to deal with new challenges: global-sized problems such as meeting future energy needs and dealing with environmental damage or designing a sustainable trade-based economy. Humanity will be unable to use its creativity and logic to build an enduring future.

Once we started digging around we saw other traits of this divide. The concept of a creative person selling out, which is a recent phenomenon, is related, as is the elitism that surrounds purity in the arts. Similarly the sciences shun anything other than obedience to existing laws, demanding compliance to theories some of which were developed many hundreds of years ago. Invention or innovation, call it what you will, but it all depends on the twin capabilities of creativity and logic. For the first time, Western education systems are actively discouraging arts and humanities courses, a fatal mistake.

We became sensitised to this issue whilst working on a series of projects that relied on collaboration between businesses, arts organisations and creative practitioners, where the debate about the role of creativity was central to our success. We became aware of the many arguments that proposed an entirely new way of working through the use of creative methods, whilst being challenged by many equally forceful arguments against such an approach. We explored examples of the management of creativity in commercial settings and found similar issues that suggested the existence of two separate worlds.

We examined the facets of subculture such as dress, language, status and lifestyles, and found differences in almost every aspect. We interviewed many creative practitioners and business managers and conducted research into the underlying causes of the divide.

We traced this divide back through history, to the industrial revolution and the demise of institutions that had given rise to the very inventions and ideas that spurred industrialisation, such as the craft guilds and the Lunar Society. We found that mechanisation, simplification and replication of menial work (mass production), colloquially known as Taylorism, seemed to be a key starting point. In the West our creative and logical capabilities were divided and the logic of science became paramount, even though it depended for its success on creative abilities. The emphasis given to left-brain logic pervaded first working practice, then education, then policy and politics. We have dubbed this the 'Lobotomy' as it metaphorically matches the division of our logical and creative thinking capacity. The consequences chime with the disastrous medical side effects of the surgery, a metaphor for many of our modern day dilemmas. In the commercial world we are struggling to solve long term problems, whilst being hung up on short term profit, and we have become focused on explaining why things have gone wrong and attributing blame. The creativity that makes us human and able to solve problems has been deliberately devalued. Consequently those that work in the creative sectors have developed a defensive elitism; many claim they find day-to-day procedural tasks difficult, tasks often dismissed as barriers to creativity. But we are capable of both. We are all human.

In this book we expose a little-understood consequence of mass production and industrialisation, and aim to answer some of the questions posed by current concerns such as the decline of transformational innovation and invention. There is some good news though. When we look around we see the beginnings of a new revolution, just as important as the industrial age. Today a few innovative companies are starting to recognise the need for creative capabilities from their employees. Many of these companies are a part of the new information age, and many are so-called 'creative industries'. A new revolution is upon us, but the old methods and thinking – or lack of it – are holding us back.

If we don't act soon, the lobotomy could become incurable. We will have created a world that is unable to invent and innovate, and we will have destroyed the precious force that has provided us with wealth, health and a longer life, with potentially disastrous consequences for our future generations.

Part 1: Chapter 2: Have you been lobotomised?

'Everything you can imagine is real.'

- Pablo Picasso

If you think there's no way a dynamic creative go-getter like you is ever going to work for those faceless corporate drones then you've probably had some form of psychological lobotomy – convinced that there are organisational skills you are not good at, that these people are not part of your world and that your creativity is your sole defining persona. Alternatively, if you believe there is no way you'd ever let those layabout arty types into your pristine office, then you too may also have been a victim. Don't think it applies to you? Some of the following questions may make you feel uncomfortable, but answer them honestly and see how you do. If you feel you live in both worlds you might want to take both sets of tests.

The following tests are designed to give you some feedback on your own attitudes. You may not have thought about these issues before, but there is no need to take a long time answering, just tick the box that feels right. The test is in two parts; one for those in more traditional blue or white collar employment, and the other for those who see themselves as creative - perhaps earning their livelihood from such activities or at least intending to. Simply tick the box that best matches your point of view. Have fun.

Table 1: Self Completion Questionnaire

Part 1 – For the Creative					
	A	B	C	D	E
	Agree	Agree Slightly	Neutr'l	Dis-agree Slightly	Dis-agree
Mainstream work					
Traditional career jobs are easy compared to a creative career					
Mainstream career jobs are often overpaid					
Blue and white collar workers are often dull					
Talking with creative people is always stimulating					
Money and people					
Most people who deal with money are corrupt					
The pursuit of money dulls real emotions					
Money gets in the way of discovering the true meaning of life					
Prioritisation					
Things just pile up. I can never seem to get on top of them.					
It doesn't matter if things are a bit late					
I often neglect close friends or family when immersed in creative work					
Creative success is more important than having a neat & tidy home and family life					
Creative work is the same as your life's work					
True happiness stems from creative activity					
There can never be enough time to achieve everything that needs to be done					
Management is a waste of time					

Part 1 - for the Creative (continued)					
	A	B	C	D	E
	Agree	Agree Slightly	Neutr'l	Dis-agree Slightly	Dis-agree
Value					
Putting a price on creative work sullies its true value					
Making a piece of art purely for profit is 'selling out' and ceases to be art					
There are positive benefits from leading a life of material hardship in the pursuit of your art form					
Creatives are not paid enough for what they do					
Creative work is often undervalued					
Agents and managers take too big a slice of the cake					
Focussing on success is a shallow goal					
Boasting about success is distasteful					
It is hard to put a price on creative work					
Creative work needs to be admired					
People are often unfairly over-critical of creative work					
Creative success stems from a strong sense of self esteem					
Training					
Training is only worth paying for if it helps to develop my creative skills					
Business management training is not something I would pay for					

Part 1 - for the creative (continued)					
	A	B	C	D	E
	Agree	Agree Slightly	Neutr'l	Dis-agree Slightly	Dis-agree
Dress and image					
Image is a key component of an artist's lifestyle					
Being individual in every way is important					
The 'high street' look is bland and unimaginative					
Charity shop clothes are a good source of a creative image					
Dealing with authority					
Staying below the radar avoids trouble					
Subverting the rules is preferable					
Authority should be challenged and confronted					
Dealing with bureaucracy					
Bureaucratic demands such as tax returns are a heavy burden					
Complaining about bureaucracy is common					
Form-filling causes stress					
It's pointless to prioritise managing personal finances					
View of others					
Making everyone feel comfortable undermines the challenges of creativity					
Those that find form-filling easy are generally not very creative					
Rich customers are really just 'punters'					
People in employment have no creative ideas					

Add up all your ticks in each column. If you scored mostly As and Bs there's a distinct possibility that your view of others has been corrupted and your world view is polarised.

If you scored predominately Ds and Es then you have a keen sense of awareness that the world is not as simple as black and white and it's important to consider all the shades of grey.

In the unlikely case that you scored mostly Cs it could be worthwhile forming some opinions either way!

How did the questions make you feel? Angry, sad or even annoyed? You can send us your scores and thoughts, and fill-in an electronic version of this test, on our website: www.lobotomybook.com.

Many of us feel we are living in both worlds - even if our work is labelled as blue collar, white collar, creative, or whatever, so why not try the non-creative questionnaire as well?

Table 2: Self completion questionnaire

Part 2 – For the Non-Creative					
	A	B	C	D	E
	Agree	Agree Slightly	Neutr'l	Dis-agree Slightly	Dis-agree
Physical appearance					
Scruffy individuals have no place in business					
I like to look smart and presentable when I'm working					
I always buy mainstream fashion goods and quality high street or smart designer clothes					
Those without money					
I view those who earn little but who work hard as a failure					
People who keep themselves poor deliberately are fools					
Dealing with Creative people					
Creative people are really hard to work with					
Creative people have no idea what real work is					
Creative people are not team players					
When negotiating a price for creative input I try to get it free or tell them it's part of their creative development					
If hiring someone creative, I will negotiate them down to the cheapest fee they will take					
I expect that creative people will always work for 'next to nothing'					
I would never ask a respectable company or individual to work for nothing					
Money represents value					

Part 2 - for the Non-Creative (continued)					
	A	B	C	D	E
	Agree	Agree Slightly	Neutr'l	Dis-agree Slightly	Dis-agree
Business world view					
Those that claim not to understand the concepts of business are foolish to follow a career that depends on it					
I have very few creative friends					
I view those who do not use professional language as childish or uneducated					
I assume that creative people do not understand what I do or how I do it					
What I do is more important than some 'off the wall' creative project					
I think most creative work is easy compared to the work I do					
I think that creatives are mostly overpaid and overvalued					
I think my ideas are just as good if not better than those of many creative people					
Value of work and rewards					
There is no point in running a business if there is no money to be made					
I work in order to earn money to enjoy myself outside of work					
Having studied for many years to gain my position, it is obvious that creatives have not worked as hard					
Business is complex creative work is not					

Part 2 continued– For the Non-Creative					
	A	B	C	D	E
	Agree	Agree Slightly	Neutr'l	Dis- agree Slightly	Dis- agree
Attitude					
I think that most creatives are lazy and difficult to work with					
My experience tells me that creatives don't listen, they tell					
A lot of creatives operate on the fringes of the law					
Creatives treat me like I'm a fool or pityingly					
A stable home and family life is more important to me than what I do for work					
I like to follow rules in life and keep within the law					
Unless others carry out similar work to me, I consider them inadequate or beneath me					
I find mixing with anyone from the creative sector unpleasant and unnerving					
I dumb down my language when talking to a 'creative person'					
When working with creative people I prefer to leave them to their thoughts and then tell them what I think of their ideas afterwards					
I think only a small handful of creatives are any good at what they do					

Total up your ticks. If the majority of them are in the A and B columns then your view of the creative marketplace, and those who work within it, may unwittingly be unfair and prejudiced.

If you scored predominately Ds and Es then you have a good sense of balance, and an awareness that the creative marketplace has an important role to play alongside business.

In the unlikely case that you scored mostly Cs it could be worth formulating some opinions either way!

How did the questions make you feel? Irritated, despairing or even irate? You can send us your scores and thoughts, and fill-in a digital version of this test, on our website: www.lobotomybook.com.

What does it all mean?

If you scored high in the As and Bs in either test you may have been at least partially affected by the lobotomy. You're suffering and may be in need of some serious help. The tests are aimed at individuals, but can also apply to organisations or groups. For example, if an organisation takes the view that creativity is just an arts issue, it may not even feature on their recruitment criteria, limiting their chances of hiring lateral free thinkers who could drive the company's evolution.

The characteristics of lobotomy are easy to spot. If the test has revealed any symptoms, you may be a victim of the lobotomising process, which ensures that the links between your creativity and logic are dulled - if not closed down altogether - causing you to live a life without one or other of your essential capabilities. The consequences are far reaching: at an individual level you may be depressed, unfulfilled or unsuccessful. If these attitudes pervade an organisation - perhaps where senior management share a similar set of views - profits may be falling, employees may be de-motivated, products or ideas may have become stale and new ideas hard to find. We've met both types of victim. At the extremes are the business people who see the world as one big market, profit as the aim, and people of little consequence. In their view creativity is mystical; certainly not part of the mainstream. What they see is numbers, targets, performance indicators and so on. They are often out of touch with their feelings and emotions and have lost contact with their creative selves. Equally, we've met the creatives who see the world of money as an evil place; who refuse to engage with mainstream commerce and rely on state benefits and grants, producing seemingly valueless art, and claiming that monetising art is selling out. They have lost contact with their logical selves. In-between are the rest of us. Many of us will be suffering the consequences of being encouraged, convinced or forced to abandon our creative capabilities, while those working in the creative sector may wonder why they are treated so badly.

So how did the lobotomy take place? How did society become relatively wealthy and successful, and at the same time begin to lose the one thing that made it happen? Why did we decide to be one or the other, but never both? Who cut the links between our creative and logical minds, and why?

Part 2: History

Part 2: Chapter 3: Cutting the wires

'Creativity is a gift. It doesn't come through if the air is cluttered.'

- John Lennon

The title of this chapter is 'cutting the wires'. We chose it for two reasons. Firstly it metaphorically replicates the surgical action taken during the practice of a medical lobotomy and secondly it represents the disconnect that contemporary western life causes inside our minds, a disconnect that divides our natural selves, causing us to favour either our creative or logical capabilities but not both.

It is worth taking a brief excursion into the world of the medical lobotomy if only to sensitise ourselves to the possibility that something that purports to be a benefit to humankind and can gain popular support is in fact the very opposite.

The story of the medical procedure of lobotomy is terrifying - a plot that would give succour to the worst horror lust of Hollywood. Unfortunately for its victims, it's true. The process involves severing the prefrontal cortex that connects the two sides of the brain, in the hope that it would cure mental illness, sometimes diagnosed because the patient was troublesome. Two men were the champions of the lobotomy, they developed it, practised it and eventually received Nobel prizes for their work. They were the Portuguese neurologist António Egas Moniz and the American neuropsychiatrist Dr. Walter Freeman.

The early version of the procedure called for holes to be drilled in the patient's head. Tissue in the frontal lobe was then destroyed by injecting alcohol. It was thought that once this connecting tissue was removed or impaired then the tensions created by conflicts between the two hemispheres of the brain would be resolved or at least abated. Later a surgical instrument was developed, known as the leucotome (or orbitoclast), to gain access to the frontal lobe through the eye sockets. You can stop reading here if this getting too excruciating. Freeman devised this method by using an ice pick and practising on grapefruit and cadavers. The leucotome was hammered into the brain through the soft bone formed by the top of the eye socket having prised the eyelid open to gain access. Once in place the blade was angled towards the white fibrous matter connecting the cortical tissue of the prefrontal cortex to the thalamus. Then the cuts were made by twisting the tool towards the nose and then back towards the brain. This was then repeated through the other eye socket.

This was taking place from 1935 until 1970, often without anaesthetic. In a BBC radio programme entitled *The Lobotomists* (29 February 2012, Radio 4) the question was asked 'How could medicine have made such a fundamental mistake?' Contemporary medical science was complicit in the adoption of a seriously flawed idea.

Moniz and Freeman popularised the procedure through the use of media, claiming unparalleled success. Following their award of the Nobel Prize for medicine in 1949 the practice went global. Follow-up research data on their patients' longer term health was sparse, and often conveniently not carried out. Had this standard medical practice been followed a gruesome picture would have emerged. Thankfully the development of drug based alternatives replaced lobotomising surgery from 1970 onwards.

So why call this book Lobotomy? Nothing so physically damaging is happening to our brains perpetrated by medical science today. However, other cultural and social forces are at work, steadily undermining our natural abilities in an attempt to neutralise our creativity or demonise our rationality. Whilst this process attempts to cut the same wires, it is reversible, something that was never true of the medical version.

Left/ Right

Something tumultuous happened to the human race in the 19th century. We decided that we had a left- or right-sided personality, depending on which part of our brain we predominantly used (although we didn't use those terms back then). This way of thinking is now discredited of course having reached a peak as the science of phrenology. Why did we do it? Was it because we needed to get really good at working in factories and on assembly lines? Getting humans to carry out repetitive tasks accurately all day long demanded a deeper understanding of the brain. Eventually being left-brained and business-like rather than right-brained with an artistic temperament became more valuable. We began to give up on the creative (right-brained) side of life and focussed instead on the serious business of standing in a line doing the same thing all day long; we even got so good at it that we invented performance measures, likening it to a sport. Time and motion studies were developed so we could spent our unique brain power working out how to do these repetitive tasks faster and faster; it even got to be called the pursuit of excellence! This is equivalent to having a semi-orbital-lobotomy - just choose which side of your brain you want to lose, you can't have both anymore - and a form of robotics was born. Once the robot human began to dominate, we built an education system to keep them coming, management processes to keep it all ticking along and burgeoning professions to keep it all in line. Now we have either creative people or non-creative people and we have creative industries or non-creative industries. We have a subculture that means the two camps are treated very differently; they find it difficult to communicate and divisions are encouraged, reinforced by group behaviours and practice. What got us to this mechanised hubris was our creativity, but now we don't seem to know what to do with it. We've run out of ideas, at a time when new ideas are paramount to our survival. Our robot selves have nothing to add. The lobotomy is almost complete, the gap between our creative and logical side has been prised wide open. It is destroying our societies by producing ever-increasing inequalities, undermining our commercial futures by reducing innovation and invention, and making us unhappy by removing our uniqueness or making life unsustainable by demeaning our rational selves. To assure ourselves that we are justified in taking up a stance as either a creative or logical person we have developed a defensive contempt for each other depending on which type of human we consider ourselves to be.

So what inhabits the gap between these two selves?

Values and beliefs: the cause of division

Our religious beliefs, social status and class, our affiliation to political parties and trade unions are all good examples of the organisational systems that inhabit the divide, with powerful allegiances being formed and groups organised to promote and protect them. The basis of the beliefs that form these groups is often historical, relevant to a time when they were a rational response to events. In some cases, the founding rationale has become diluted by new knowledge or changes in economic circumstances - for example, does it still make sense to organise labour as a collective to bargain with employers? It was entirely appropriate as the industrial revolution took hold, but in the information age - when more and more jobs are created in the professions and hi-tech companies on a short-term basis - is there a better way to manage this? Other means may be more appropriate, bringing increased flexibility such as arranging bargaining through agents. Similarly, companies organised around hierarchies, formal roles and rules - and designed to maximise profits - may not be appropriate when the impact on our well-being and environment is gaining in importance. However, once these belief systems (sometimes referred to as memes, a term coined in 1976 by Richard Dawkins in *The Selfish Gene*[1]) become engrained, they become difficult to change and to challenge, even if they appear arcane and unworldly in the context of a new modernity. Memes have properties similar to genes, that is: they self-replicate, mutate and are subject to change through external forces. However, unlike genes, memes are used to transfer cultural beliefs. They represent a societal 'gene' that has become part of our interactive DNA.

In the field of creative endeavour, we may also find elements of these memes – for instance, beliefs in rules or the promotion of behaviours that appear to be based on some shared philosophy that claims ownership of 'the right way of doing things'. Memes can be viewed as helpful or harmful depending on their alignment with the current economic and political direction. For example in a world where arts are liberalised and open to all, a harmful meme could be 'purity of the arts' or the assumption that creatives are difficult to manage. Equally the development of a meme that suggests arts-based education is of less value than science or that employability is the measure to judge a subject's worth, implies that all humans are non-individuals, that is blank slates with no preferences and can be utilised at will to meet the demands of commerce. The European Enlightenment and the Age of Reason were not promoted by industrial or commercial concerns; these two civilising movements were the result of philosophical, moral and political reasoning, drawing on history, science and a new found literacy combined with a technology of communication. The success and immense changes that occurred were predominantly rooted in the domain of the humanities. There are dangerous consequences of a narrow focus on consumerism and wealth at the expense of the arts and humanities.

These sorts of harmful values and beliefs that are associated with non-logical work today are a reversal of earlier values. For example, during the late Middle Ages, craft guilds developed as an essential component of economic growth. They represented crafts and skills of every type: stonemasons, carpenters, clock makers, glass makers and painters. An artist, or painter, could progress from journeyman to master over the course of several years, and would accept many commissions as well as paint his or her own ideas. Compare the explicit creative craftsmanship embodied in Venice; the buildings, furniture, glassware and clothing preserved to this day, with any modern city. Where has the craftsmanship gone?

Craft guilds, industrialisation and art elitism

In the Middle Ages, history tells us that guilds were much more than organising economic entities. There was a respect between the guilds, a wider community role and a moral purpose. There was certainly no divide between creative craft skills and business in terms of the value of each. These skills were shared and integrated. There was no barrier to selling products or associating with philanthropists or sponsors, and there was certainly no concept of 'selling out'. Creative or craft based work was never thought of as devalued by producing what was popular and offering it for sale. Creative craft skills were highly valued; there was no attitude or bigotry associated with those who earned their living through their creative endeavours. However challenges to this status quo arose during industrialisation. Guilds were criticised in the 18th and 19th centuries for holding back progress and acting as cartels. The industrial revolution with its growth of factories and the development of large scale machinery, meant employers wanted workers who would carry out repetitious simple tasks for little pay. The working methods developed to enable this became known as *Taylorism* (also known as scientific management), named after its inventor and main protagonist Fredrick Winslow Taylor, a 19th century American Quaker. The main aim of this application of scientific methods to work was to transform craft production into mass production, and thereby enable knowledge transfer between and from workers into tools, processes, and documentation: the antithesis of the craft guild values. To facilitate development of these workflows, time and motion studies were developed to find the most productive methods. A new class system was born, clearly defined by tasks, abilities, roles and status. There was little room for the craft guilds or their values in the new world. Peter Drucker observed of Taylor:

> Frederick W. Taylor was the first man in recorded history who deemed work deserving of systematic observation and study. On Taylor's 'scientific management' rests, above all, the tremendous surge of affluence in the last 75 years which has lifted the working masses in the developed countries well above any level recorded before, even for the well-to-do. Taylor, though the Isaac Newton (or perhaps the Archimedes) of the science of work, laid only first foundations, however. Not much has been added to them since – even though he has been dead all of sixty years[2].

Taylor worked in the factories and applied his creativity to the problem of how to improve production. His methods led to the possibilities of automation and the adoption of digital information technologies. Meanwhile, the creative sector found its values challenged and its economic worth in the new world questioned.

In the 18th and 19th centuries elitism in the arts became a part of an artist's experience. For example the new French impressionists had a hard time convincing the Académie des Beaux-Arts that their art was worthy of exhibition. A panel of peers would deliberate on any painting and accept or reject it, particularly if it did not meet any of the main criteria for acceptable art – for example, religious images were particularly favoured. Many notable painters were rejected: - Claude Monet, Pierre-Auguste Renoir, Alfred Sisley, Frédéric Bazille, Camille Pissarro, Paul Cézanne, and Armand Guillaumin, names that are revered today. Similar vetting bodies were established in music and other forms of artistic expression. The aesthetic value of the arts, rather than the financial value, gained ground, and even today this attitude is still prevalent within the creative classes –in direct opposition to the non-creatives' view in which famous paintings are judged by how much they sell for. This also holds true for the works of contemporary artists such as Warhol, Hirst and Koons, who experimented with embracing Taylorist processes, but only really succeeded in aping mass-production methods. Their final product is still hung in galleries as art for the elite with enormous price tags.

Traits of elitism in the arts can be found within national sponsoring bodies such Arts Council England (ACE). Their guidance for grants applications for moving image excludes TV pilots, video and film projects. Don't bother to apply if you're interested in any of these:

- Film production, including the development or production of narrative shorts or features, pilots for television series, or documentaries on the arts
- Mainstream animation, e.g. conventional character-based narrative, cartoons, television pilots and script development
- Support for screenwriting projects or script development for film and television
- Stand-alone documentation projects
- Promotional films and videos

If we attach such values to creative products, then those that must live by them are empowered to think that way too. That is, they may imagine that they are working in an environment that rewards purity and peer group approval, prioritising reviews, praise and tributes above financial value or marketability of their product. While these may all be part and parcel of success, without financial support they begin to rely on patronage, either through the state or through wealthy individuals or groups. Instead of being part of the central economic activity, as they were under the craft guild system, they become disposable, unnecessary and unimportant and difficulties justifying their existence arise. No wonder then that when an economic depression arrives, the arts are often the hardest hit. Back in 2011, in response to the last economic downturn, ACE suffered a 25% cut in its budget, representing the largest cut suffered by any UK government body at that time, and it has since implemented more cuts. Local English councils also took the axe to the arts, with some city councils planning to cut *all* of their arts budgets. Shackled by elitist values and purist claims, the creative community have found it impossible to marshal a viable and acceptable argument that demonstrates the social, economic, political and technological value of their work. If they continue this practice not only will their own opportunities be stunted but the needs of orthodox business to engage with creative workers will be unmet.

Both sides need to change. Taylorism has improved productivity in terms of industrial production, but one damaging consequence is that a vital creative community essential to our future well-being is being left out.

This environment has left many arts-based companies in England relying on grants made available through the state. Similar models have been established elsewhere, where funding is provided either through private donations, or state funding. However some are now turning to the new crowdfunding model, which is a patronage system involving many small private backers. In the US the balance is heavily tipped towards private funding, with the National Endowment for the Arts (NEA) offering around $100m per year, whilst private donations exceed $12 billion. This is not to say this patronage model is right or wrong; it may well be the only way that the arts and many creative skills could have survived and grown faced with the de-skilling imposed by the industrial revolution. However, the consequences of creating a dual marketplace with different value systems (where mass commercial artists and art are devalued and elitist fine art is highly valued yet rarely financially rewarded) may explain why we have developed a divided view of the world of work and rewards.

For those that do not engage in creative work as a mainstay of their livelihood, these values can look obtuse. Certainly, it can be difficult to convince conventional taxpayers, who work for an employer in a regular job, that their taxes or donations from profits should be used to pay someone else to carry out creative activities. The product of these activities – a play, a painting, a sculpture, may not be something they wish to engage with. For voters this funding mechanism may appear valueless and seemingly devoid of any return, and certainly open to challenge.

As we have seen, the seeds of this division between the two groups were sown in the industrialisation of the 18th and 19th centuries, and the subsequent progressive era that swept away many of the memes of the earlier forms of social and economic development. The industrial revolution was a product of creativity but, paradoxically, one of its legacies may well be the marginalisation of this essential human ability.

Creativity under attack

The following headline appeared as part of a review of a recent research paper aimed at understanding creative individuals: *'Creatives are drug abusers and criminals'*[3]. Swedish researchers at the Karolinska Institute found that writers had a higher risk of anxiety and bipolar disorders, schizophrenia, unipolar depression, and substance abuse. They conclude that creative individuals were twice as likely to commit suicide.

This isolation of the creative individual as a form of dangerous human was reinforced elsewhere. Francesca Gino of Harvard Business School and Dan Ariely of Duke University presented evidence that highly creative people are more likely to engage in unethical activities, apparently because they are better at finding ways to justify such behaviour[4].

Reduce this down to a snappy media headline in today's sensationalist world and we should not be too surprised by 'Creatives are drug abusers and criminals'.

This is just the tip of a large and forbidding iceberg. The 'disease' - or prejudice - has spread into our institutions, policies, processes, systems, language and lifestyles. All are corroded by the division into one camp or the other.

This may not matter of course were it not for the innovation crisis. You may not believe that such a crisis exists, after all there are new web sites published every day, new ways of consuming, new apps for our phones, 3D printing, graphene based surface materials and so on, but these technologies are simply improvements on existing technologies. Ignore the media hype, they aren't revolutionary in the same way as Turing's first computer, the use of electricity for lighting and heating or the first steam powered locomotive.

Recent research in the US shows that creativity is in decline[5]. Combine this fact with research that shows only 9% of institutions in the US conducted any R&D between 2006 and 2011[6] and you get a very worrying situation. Mix in economic stagnation (Europe and The USA are experiencing flat economic growth) and ask where the new big ideas are and you can see how the lobotomy is causing havoc. Having demoted creativity to an arts only activity and made sure rewards are skewed towards short term financial game plays and away from new thinking, pretty soon the gravy train is leaving the rails. Getting it hitched up again so we're all on board might take a generation... or more.

So what happens when we divide our people into one camp or the other? What attitudes and behaviours can we expect?

Walking the talk

We interviewed the managing director of an established training and development company that conducts creative role-play activities within large organisations. The aim of the company is to enable business change. He has a background in theatre and he decided to explore the corporate market to test his ideas for inspirational training using creative methods. One of the many projects his company carried out involved working with a large telecoms supplier to sensitise their staff to the issues and new legislation concerning racial equality. The project was instigated by a forward thinking human resources team, who were very aware of the legacy problems they had among their engineering workforce. The objective was to reduce the incidence of racial prejudice in the workplace.

They employed professional actors to facilitate the role-play. Scenes were designed and enacted that highlighted the consequences of prejudice, followed by a discussion with the staff who took part. His observations were revealing. Many of the actors had little understanding of life inside a large corporation. They were unsympathetic towards the people within the organisations they were working with, (who were often antagonistic towards participating in role-play). The actors' main motivation for taking part in such activities was financial, to support their work in the arts. However the same actors would gladly work for very little or no pay, provided it was a dramatic production in a theatre setting or as part of a film. Sometimes they thought the people they worked with were from 'another world'; they practised a kind of snobbery towards these non-creative workers. To ensure the dramatic piece was successful a go-between was required, someone who could interpret requirements in 'business speak' and re-present this to the creative freelancers in a language they would understand.

This role fell to trained business facilitators, including the managing director, who were invited to meetings with prospective clients. The MD's comments confirm the difficulty: 'Coming from the arts – the first impression of the corporate workplace is often that it is incomprehensible. Artists may not have experienced office life and its associated rules, social codes and working environments.

'I began to realise how hard these people's lives were, compared to mine. They were expected to be at their desks every day, limited time off (holidays), constrained to follow directions from a superior, often working in fear of losing their jobs, and many did not seem to enjoy what they were doing. They all wore similar clothes and used language that made it difficult for anyone from outside to understand what they wanted'.

After several small contracts where he scripted and ran the workshops himself, he began to expand his new business by hiring others and scaling up the work.

'I realised I would have to translate. The freelancers were like me, this was a world foreign to all of us, but I had begun to understand what they were trying to achieve'.

The impact was to change his view of the way people who did not earn a living through their creative skills were forced to live.

'I began to have real sympathy for people in the business community – and this fed into my creative theatre work - I learnt that audiences were not a homogenous crowd but individuals who had made an effort in their stressed lives to come and support my work'.

It is always heartening to hear that it is possible to gain an understanding of both sides, but not all such meetings have such a positive outcome.

Sue, one of the authors of this book, worked as a Creative Director of a UK government-sponsored programme aimed at developing collaborative creative projects in schools. She was attending a meeting to discuss the details of a forthcoming arts festival. The aim of these events was to engage and inspire young people, many of whom lived in an area of economic deprivation. It was proposed that these young people would be invited to take part in creative activities as part of the festival. The discussion ranged over what projects could be run that would meet the requirements of the programme. Sue made it clear that the projects would need to be measurable in some way, and that this was a precondition to funding. This was greeted with derision by the creative community – 'that's just the sort of remark we would expect from you lot' they sang sarcastically, raising their eyes to heaven and shaking their heads. They made it clear that any such approach would undermine their creative ideas. Sue left the meeting feeling excluded, insulted and annoyed. Funding ambitions were hardy well served by this level of behaviour.

In contrast creative practitioners (craftsmen and women) may feel puzzled and angry by the way they are treated. For example consider this blog post[7]: *It is simple: why do clients not value our work?*

'I can liken the current scenarios I am facing to, oh I don't know, let's say I am a chip shop owner. So I am busy frying up some delicious chips, I have worked hard at my business and I pride myself on producing the best quality bag of fries for miles around. I should be good at it, I've spent years perfecting the best-fried chip. A customer walks in,

"'Bag of chips, please". "Not a problem, here you go, that's £1.50," I might say. "£1.50?!," the customer retorts. "I was thinking more like 20p, that's value for money, isn't it?"

'Would anyone tell a chip shop owner that their chips are worth significantly less than they are? Would you go into, say, an

accountant's office, and tell them they're only worth £7 an hour? Would you ask someone to do some work for you for nothing and feel like you were doing them a favour???

'I hasten to add that in a scenario whereby I am being asked to do jobs, and I offer a quote (that is significantly less than what I feel is appropriate) that is then sent back with the line "I didn't think it was going to cost this much, I'll do it myself", is not unusual. In fact, it has happened to me at least four times in the last week. I wonder if it is just me facing these challenges. I can't be the only one.

'I value what I do highly. I have many, many years experience in creativity and business, have hundreds of successful projects under my belt and yet, people see me as a very talented volunteer. Do we all value our work or do we sell out? Why is it that people think they are doing me a favour by asking me to do something for nothing, or for very little? Are designers and artists regarded as unnecessary? How do we find those who do value our work? *'If you know the secret, be kind and let me know. I am frustrated, angry and ready to give up*

.

Connecting up again

To begin to close the gap there is a need to look at the way modern businesses are developing. In sectors such as animation filmmaking and information technology the 'gurus' behind these enterprises do not have time to debate the creativity versus knowledge script. They have set up work cultures that promote both capabilities because they know they need both. Anyone wanting to be part of this new joined up world needs to start there.

At the end of this book you'll find numerous ideas for getting back in touch with whatever part of you has been lost. We also include unique organisational ideas to kick-start the repair work in companies and institutions. But change without policy intervention will be piecemeal. It starts here and now, so look deep within yourself and your organisations to fix it.

In conclusion

Our modern economic and social environment has traits that undermine creativity and innovation and thereby sustainable successful business. This is damaging because our future depends on our creative and logical abilities working together. Without action, we will be overwhelmed by our problems. Each generation will begin to decline as the fabric of our success is worn thin by the reuse of known solutions that can't provide the impetus they once did. It is going to get tougher to survive, there are big problems out there that won't go away without new ideas and the savvy to make them work.

Part 2: Chapter 4: The scale of the problem

'If the doors of perception were cleansed everything would appear to man as it is, infinite'.

- William Blake

We are in trouble.

Next time you have a good view over any city take a look and imagine life without creativity. Imagine that some virus is at work which gradually removes all human creativity in reverse order. Your laptop and mobile phone vanish, computers and the internet are eliminated. Planes fall from the sky, cars, buses, trains all come to a halt, ships sink and the edges of cities begin to recede. Schools, hospitals, houses and churches all collapse and roads, electricity pylons and railways melt away. Shops, stadiums, pubs, restaurants, cafes and libraries all crumble to dust; books blow away in the wind. Hats, umbrellas, shoes, suits, jeans, socks, coats, shirts fall apart. Bread, butter, beer, wine are all gone. Medicines disappear and all oil based fuel evaporates. Anything made of metal vanishes. Every household product or tool you have ever used will be gone. You too will begin to feel differently; your view of the future will shrink until only the present will be apparent. Your ability to imagine will focus on immediate problems, and you will lose access to your knowledge about science, technology, art, music, history, geography and philosophy. Only your most basic skills will remain. Soon all that will be left of your world is plant life and animals. Finally, you will lose the ability to do anything other than prioritise food and shelter, but without any tools, weapons or armour, you will no longer be the top-of-the-food-chain predator, you will be the prey - you will be food.

As we begin the 21st century we have some large global problems to deal with, and our track record of taking action is looking woeful.

There are environmental threats to our planet, and consequentially to our way of life. There are many unresolved, long-running, damaging wars and conflicts, the scale and depth of which are seemingly beyond our capabilities to solve. We face an energy crisis, a population crisis and recently we seem to have lost the ability to manage our economies and our financial markets. Our trust in these institutions is subsiding, being replaced with cynicism and doubt. On the up-side we have new technologies, many brought to us by the internet, and there are new less damaging ideas for energy production. Knowledge is shared more widely than ever. If we need some information quickly we can start with Google and Wikipedia, the former even becoming a verb. We crave sensible decisions that will provide a sustainable future together with ethical and moral leadership, but these seem hard to find as our political dogfights degenerate year after year into polarised extremism.

Creativity, a concept which is difficult to define, underpins everything we do and how we solve our problems, yet in the West we ascribe it little value. We confuse it with art or consider it the domain of a minority of weird people. Creative behaviour can equally well be applied to science (think Albert Einstein or Leonardo Da Vinci) and business (think Apple Corporation or Amazon). It may have an intangible outcome, such as a new thought or idea rather than a song, a computer game or new invention. Yet we ignore it as a defining human trait and fail to nurture it in our children. Instead we insist on repetition, feeding them a diet of facts and hoping they will do well in tests. These tests leave our young people with the impression that all problems have a multiple choice answer that can be selected from a list. Well, as we know, the real world just isn't like that. We expect the future to be better, but actively undermine the one thing that made the past successful. Our education systems have become a memory game, our uniqueness is stifled and truly original thinking goes unrewarded - at least until the higher levels of education, by which time it is too late for most. Divergent thinking, a natural ability that all children have, is now largely crushed by the age of 14, thanks to our maniacal belief in the past as a way to the future.

In the business world diversification, a key component of natural evolution, is being marginalised, and innovation is effectively discouraged by our litigation systems. As American legal scholar Tim Wu describes in his sobering book, *The Master Switch: The Rise and Fall of Information Empires*[8], the one thing that now features in every successful company is patent litigation - thus significantly narrowing the field of creative opportunities available.

The real engine of economic prosperity is not the large companies that exist now; it is the companies that will exist in the future. They, and what they do, have not been invented yet, and without the human capacity to create, they never will. We need people who can imagine the future, start companies and build a better world, whether it be through the generation of green energy or through advances in engineering, medical science or information technology. You might imagine that you need to have a university degree, a master's qualification or maybe a PhD to be able to do this - but some of today's most successful innovative companies, such as Twitter and Facebook, have an interesting common denominator in that their founders were all college drop-outs, they chose to leave the education system to be able to explore their new ideas.

Leaving aside the groups who favour extreme 'back to basics' cave-life as a sustainable future, how do we understand, perceive, react to, utilise and manage creativity and creativeness in an effective way? This is a modern question. It arises when designing an education curriculum, developing new products in business and dealing with unique problems and decision making in politics. When we mismanage creativity it can encourage antagonistic philosophies (creativity v logic) and shape emotive, valueless arguments, leaving future generations unprepared to deal with inevitable problems caused by our success. Today civilisations are considered to be organisations that display continual complexity. This state is sometimes referred to as living at the 'edge of chaos'. Dealing with this powerful storm requires ingenuity: a combination of creativity and logic. An impoverished future awaits unless we take action to rebalance these two key human attributes.

Whilst we can recognise the economic and social risks we must also accept that the battle between creativity and logic has given rise to an insidious social intolerance. As we have seen, creative and non-creative people are often stereotyped, leading to discriminatory behaviour between and against the creative/non-creative groups, feeding a form of social bigotry whilst fuelling divisive policy making, draining resources and undermining human progress. Those in creative careers often complain of being undervalued, while those in non-creative careers complain of boredom. We are not the first to address this question but we may be the first to ask why it should still be an important question at the turn of the 21st century - what has happened, how did we get to such a strange understanding of our natural abilities and how can we undo the damage?

As we have noted, in the West, the term creativity tends to be associated with the arts. Set up a Google alert for creativity and 90% of the results are arts based, but try the same thing for innovation and 90% are business based, or try invention which delivers a predominantly science based result. The amount of investment directed at business innovation or scientific invention and research is staggering. There is virtually no investment in creativity.

But how can innovation or invention appear without creativity? Creativity is found and expressed in collaborative and collective as well as individual activities, in teamwork and organisations, in communities and in governments. It is not unique to the arts. It is fundamental to advances in the sciences, mathematics, technology, politics, business and all areas of everyday life, but its association with the arts is now persistent.

Creativity is sometimes viewed as applying to only a few exceptional people with unusual talents. This implies elitism and undermines the global value of creativity for all of us, and is often used to dissuade policy makers from investing in this capability. Undoubtedly, there are people with exceptional creative gifts, but everyone is capable of creative achievement in some area of activity, provided the conditions are right and they have acquired the relevant knowledge and skills.

So if you're looking for that spark of creativity in your workforce don't be surprised when none appears. They had their lights turned out long ago, toiling in the dark mines of education.

Fixing this will take a change of perspective.

Changing perspectives

On September 23, 1973, American Indian activist and chief of the Indian Chippewa tribe Adam Fortunate Eagle (born Adam Nordwall[9]), dressed in full regalia, landed in Rome and claimed possession of Italy 'by right of discovery' just as Christopher Columbus had claimed America nearly 500 years earlier. 'I proclaim this day the day of the discovery of Italy', he said.

'What right', asked the chief, 'did Columbus have to discover America when it had already been inhabited for thousands of years? The same right that I have to come now to Italy and proclaim the discovery of your country'[10].

This might seem like a crazy idea, but of course this is how America was 'discovered'. What Adam Fortunate Eagle was trying to do was to try and reverse people's perspective and get them to see how it felt to be an American Indian.

Understanding someone else's point of view is key to reversing the

Lobotomy. The stereotypes associated with so-called left- and right-brained people - and the consequent negative assumptions and reactions - are perspectives that can be corrected. What is clear is that these destructive assumptions have a common root cause, one that is familiar in other areas of life. They are, in short, a form of prejudice.

To be on the receiving end of prejudice is to be subjected to disrespectful attitudes, or excluded unfairly, or made a joke of, or insulted and ignored. Applied in the context of the creative and non-creative cultures it includes traits of bullying and arrogance. At its worst it can manifest itself as a prejudice as destructive as any other. It can mean that a career is abandoned, or a critical opportunity lost, the potential new ideas left untested and the solutions ignored. As the old adage says 'If you do what you've always done you'll get what you've always got'.

So it seems sensible to be impartial, even-handed and fair-minded when dealing with others. We should be able to work with diverse skilled groups to solve problems without excluding them for prejudicial reasons. So why does prejudice happen?

Categorical thinking

The roots of prejudice lie at the heart of our everyday decision making. We are programmed to categorise and prioritise, polarising everything: night and day, good and bad, black and white. But these categories are just the ends of a continuous scale. It is convenient to use categories, it speeds up decision making. It is much easier to gauge what to wear if the weather is cold or hot, because having to estimate the actual temperature then find suitable clothing would take a long time, so we estimate, categorise and decide quickly. In other words, we use categorical thinking to help us make judgements. Once we have defined our categories we apply them to help us plan our daily strategies; we process vast amounts of information every second. Is this person trustworthy or suspicious? The answer helps us decide what action to take immediately. Unfortunately, we build stereotypes on the basis of these categories. Once we have identified the category we apply attitudes, values and beliefs to it. As we've seen, this aids quick decision making, based on immediate judgements, 'thinking without thinking' as Malcolm Gladwell described in his book, *Blink*[11]. This is a very useful human skill; however, it can be dangerous. Preconceptions about people based on false categorisations and associated attitudes lead to prejudice. To illustrate this, look at the following diagram which we have adapted from the web article *understanding prejudice*[12].

Mike   *... Sue*

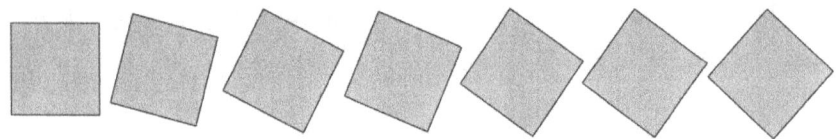

The boxes at either end are easily definable. On the left we have a square, and on the right a diamond, but what are the shapes between them? They clearly exist but we don't have a category for them – we might say that they're a square on its side, or a square leaning at 15 degrees. To illustrate the danger of predicting categories 'without thinking', consider a definition of these shapes in terms of career types. Lets say that someone whose career is spent working in a formal office setting, such as Mike, could be thought of as a 'square' and they are likely to have traits associated with squares. These could involve:

- Wearing a business suit, or some other form of formal dress, together with a moderate or conservative hair style.
- Using complex 'business speak'.
- Having a numerate job and using business software to manage tasks and communicate.

- Working progressively through a number of ordered tasks and being involved in team meetings through their day.
- Having a defined start and end time for their work and having a shared vision of the organisation they work for.

At the other end we recognise a diamond. In this case we may imagine someone like Sue, who might typically:

- Work in a creative setting, possibly in a workshop or studio.
- Dress in a flamboyant or unusual style.
- Use specialist, 'niche' language.
- Use graphics and design software on a computer.
- Work alone throughout most of the day, and not work though pre-set tasks, or attend team meetings.
- Not have defined start and end times and is personally involved with the value of her work.

In effect, we have defined two stereotypes. If these are embedded in our understanding of the world - that is, we know only about squares and diamonds - then all the other boxes have to become one or the other. If that is the case, when we meet someone new we ask are they a square or a diamond? We may associate other traits with these stereotypes that have been suggested by media or through conversations within our peer groups; for example we may have negative beliefs that squares are boring, are emotionally challenged, unable to express themselves and are primarily interested in money, or that diamonds are prone to drink and drug abuse, are lazy, unable to organise themselves or make a decent living. Of course, neither of these descriptions would actually fit either Mike or Sue. We may have based our snap decision on the basis of what that person was wearing, or what they said, or the context of our meeting. However, our snap decision on whether someone is a square or a diamond can have far more damaging consequences, particularly if we are not in the same group[13].

I'm in with the 'In crowd'[14]

This popular hit record of the 60s and 70s eloquently described our desire to be part of the fashionable, attractive and acceptable. The 'in' crowd is another way of describing groups that are beneficial for us to belong to. But what if you are excluded? What if you are part of the 'out' crowd?

Another component of prejudicial behaviour is known as the 'outgroup homogeneity' effect. Simply put, those who are not part of our immediate peer group are viewed as all being pretty much the same (having homogenous traits), whereas those within our 'in group' are viewed as having a diverse set of skills.

This is because we are regularly sensitised to the skills and other traits of the people we work with all the time, but we don't have that intimate knowledge of those we don't spend time with, so we tend to lump everyone else together into a large homogeneous category - hence phrases such as 'men are all the same' or 'football supporters are all thugs'.

To test this effect, researchers at Princeton University asked students in four different 'eating clubs' to rate members of their own club and the three other clubs on various personality scales such as *introverted to extroverted* and *arrogant to humble*. The results showed that all the students tended to rate members of their own club as more varied in personality than those in the other clubs ('outgroups')[15].

Prejudice occurs when we look around our 'in crowd' and think the only people who have any real, valid skills are those who are in our clique, either virtually or physically. This can look different depending on whether we are examining a creative environment or a more formal business workplace. In a creative career setting, physical interaction between different groups may rarely take place.

The creative ingroup may be loosely aligned, because in many cases it is made up of small operations – one or two individuals, or several freelance operatives collaborating on a project for a brief period. This can lead to a classic ingroup/outgroup situation, with some powerful imbalances in terms of scale and strength of relationships. By contrast the more conventional formal business ingroups are much larger, and have much closer and longer lasting interdependent working methods. There is a much stronger force for outgroup prejudice present within these large, long lasting ingroup clusters.

The consequence of thinking that everyone in an outgroup is the same (outgroup homogeneity), is termed ingroup favouritism. Many forms of bias and prejudice develop not because you despise the outgroup, but because the positive emotions of sympathy, trust, and admiration are reserved for your ingroup members.

Ingroup bias can develop quickly and become embedded in actions and reactions. Henri Tajfel invented what is now known as the 'minimal group procedure'[16], an experimental technique in which people who have never met before are divided into groups on the basis of minimal information (e.g., a preference for one colour versus another, or even just the toss of a coin). What Tajfel discovered is that groups formed on the basis of almost *any* distinction are prone to ingroup bias. Within minutes of being divided into groups, people tend to see their collective as superior to others and will seek to maintain an advantage over them. Beyond the experiment it is easy to recognise this type of behaviour. A member of a strong financial group or society who becomes bankrupt will be viewed with some sympathy within their group, whereas a similar individual as a member of an outgroup may be viewed as both a failure and as the architect of his or her own demise.

Here is a chilling example of what we are referring to[17]. When the Jews were first forced to flee their homeland some 2,500 years ago, they were not allowed to own land or become artisans in the new regions in which they settled. Needing a livelihood, some took to lending money, one of the few professions to which they were allowed access. Although this choice of occupation was an accidental by-product of restrictive laws, it led to a dispositional attribution about Jews: that they were interested only in dealing with money and not in 'honest' skilled labour, like farming. This stereotype contributed greatly to the barbaric consequences of European anti-Semitism during the 1930s and 1940s and has persisted to this day.

At its extreme this attitude to outgroups can lead to genocide. This is justified by blaming the target group for some societal malaise then de-humanising them. They become 'vermin' and 'must be exterminated so that the ideological vision can be achieved. Hitler, Stalin and Mao Tse Tung employed this strategy to convince their populations that millions of their fellow citizens should be murdered.

Not only do ingroup members attribute causes of failure using double standards, they also view success differently. A positive outgroup success is viewed as a fluke or a one-off or luck. This makes it virtually impossible for outgroup members to break free of the prejudices they face, because their positive actions are explained away while their failures and shortcomings are used against them. For example, regardless of how much positive work a politician may do helping the poor or championing environmental issues, should they have an extra marital affair they may be immediately and irrevocably tainted as an untrustworthy philanderer.

The mass media is saturated with images of stereotypes. They are used to sell products, enliven drama and spice up news. The sheer volume of advertising suggests that many people are exposed to multiple stereotypes on a daily basis. Advertisements occupy almost 60% of newspaper space, 52% of magazine pages, 35% of online content, 18% of radio time, and 17% of primetime television[18]. With such an avalanche of suggestive content no wonder our prejudices get in the way of 'real world' decisions. Add to this the deliberate manufacture of sensational copy to feed the internet 'page-view' based blogging industry, which is unverified and unregulated, and groups and individuals are soon demonised. Once demonised little opportunity is offered for their defence.

Overcoming these negative group dynamics is important. Actively engaging with other groups to enrich ideas avoids stagnation. A wide diversity of ideas brings informed options, and these can lead to better solutions. Networking among groups is an activity that enables diversity and broader knowledge sharing.

The 'Goldilocks' network - how networks can stifle or encourage creativity

We've seen how far the Lobotomy can penetrate our daily lives by encouraging the invisible enemy, prejudice. This is quickly established and reinforced by media interest groups that attempt to influence our judgements and decisions. However, becoming members of groups is part of our natural desire to belong. There are evolutionary/tribal forces that encourage us to join and they provide us with confirmation and authority, impart status and provide recognition of who we are. These groups are essential, forming important collective interaction points that make up our societies. They act as communicators and aggregators and make civilisation possible[19]. Even if a group attempts to exist entirely outside mainstream society, some form of communication is inevitable, which may begin with the use of a science such as electricity, exchange of goods or use of the Internet. These groups interact in a variety of networks, which can have a positive or negative effect on our creative productivity and eventually our long term well-being and sustainability.

Today many of us are associated with colleagues, friends and family through social networks, but these have characteristics that can either encourage or discourage collaboration and creativity. New positive outcomes may emerge if the collaboration is in the best interest of all participants. A recent article in the *New Scientist*[20] magazine used the term the 'Goldilocks Network' to highlight the features of networks that lead to creative success.

Ingroup networks are unsurprisingly bad at encouraging creativity if they operate in a closed way. The most effective models are those that are more open, where members also belong to other diverse groups. This diversity serves to uproot ideas from one group to create a new idea that may be shared or planted within the other groups, although this interconnectedness cuts both ways. If there are too many familiar connections, nothing new is likely to emerge. If there are too many diverse connections, inspiration can be low. There appears to be an optimal model or form where the members of these groups form a 'superhub' that brings together ideas from each smaller group. In this way, being an outsider with many links to unconnected networks allows ideas to flow, whereas being a member of a familiar network has the opposite effect. This theory fits well with the way creative networks operate[21] and explains why closed groups (ingroups) are bad for creativity and tolerance. Closed ingroups not only engender prejudice, but also prevent creativity taking place; ideas can't germinate if there is nowhere for them to grow.

Historic examples of such creative networks include those formed by the French Impressionists, who inspired surrealism, and The Lunar Society: a loose collective initiated by Erasmus Darwin (the grandfather of Charles Darwin) which also included Mathew Boulton, the business partner of James Watt (the inventor of the steam engine), Josiah Wedgewood the English pottery manufacturer and Joseph Priestley the philosopher and dissenting churchman as well as many eminent politicians and academics - as a prototype of a modern think tank, such as the UK-based Demos[22]. The individual members certainly changed the world, but not on their own.

Groups such as the Lunar Society and its modern equivalents enable change and progress. They provide a forum to develop vision and discuss pragmatic planning. For example to build the railways, factors such as new company formations, equity funding, steel manufacture, land acquisition, government support, new legal frameworks, media interest, people's votes, and many more aspects, all needed to come together to create that revolution in transport. Once this was achieved, smaller incremental improvements could then be made. Although we may wonder at the modernity of rail transport today, a high-speed electric train is still a train. Similarly, the Internet is based on technologies that were created between the 1950s and 1970s. Since then many valuable incremental improvements have been made; layer upon layer of software and better hardware has been added, all basically following the same rules, until today it gives the appearance of a revolutionary change every few months, but in fact under the hood there is nothing so revolutionary going on.

So where are the modern world-changing networks to be found? We should be experiencing an upsurge of ideas and new products, as the internet provides ample opportunities to network with anyone - but this is not the case. There are collective discussion groups such as TED[23] (Technology, Entertainment, Design) although their power to influence the world is muted perhaps by their aims, which are simply to spread ideas. Similarly new 'Lunar' societies have sprung up in England and Australia, although their aims appear to be localised or educational, rather than transformational. Instead, patent challenges and small amendments to existing products are becoming the norm. This point is ably discussed by John Naughton in the Sunday *Observer*.[24] He brings together the evidence that shows that the well has run dry. All that's left are a series of small incremental changes; the innovation of the Internet is over and now all we see is just another web-based 'me too' business model, such as Kickstarter (one of a number of crowd-funding sites) or another app to download to the smartphone; small beer in the world transformation stakes.

Whatever the internet may have created, it is not working to encourage new world-changing ideas, although it has provided an effective channel to support incremental improvement.

Water water everywhere

Samuel Taylor Coleridge found a way to describe the frustration of thirst despite the availability of plentiful water in his poem *The Rime of the Ancient Mariner* which contains the immortal line, 'water water everywhere nor any drop to drink' (He was recounting the experience of being becalmed at sea). We have a world full of creative, rational people and yet we do not allow them to behave in this way; instead, we have split their natural collaborative capacity in two and excluded one from the other. We have designed a world that encourages division and favours the rational and logical over the creative. In order to slake our cultural thirst, creative networks need to operate in the same way as individuals should - without barriers. Instead, these networks are operating without fuel for the engine: innovation without creativity. The ability to use all of our capacity is corrupted by the lobotomy. Networks only interact with others that display similar traits. A network that used to function quite naturally, with multiple disciplines interacting to fertilise inventiveness, is now stymied. Like our brains, it functions best when everything is connected.

It lives

The lobotomy is demonstrably real. Everyday experiences are all too familiar.

Mike writes: Whilst I was working for a new UK business, a director was appointed to interface with the financial sector at a senior level. Her personal style consisted of bright clothes and ostentatious shoes and she sported vivid, dyed hair. Whilst she had the pedigree to take on such a role, she was often ignored at conferences, and her voice was lost at meetings. Outside the office others began to talk about her in less than complimentary terms. Despite her qualifications, her appearance and demeanour were enough to stimulate exclusion reactions from a powerful 'ingroup' culture. In another role, I was asked to lead a discussion about 'business performance measurement' among a group of creative practitioners: artists, writers and actors. They made no effort to understand any of the concepts I was putting forward, even those based on elementary mathematics, because they believed that the use of numerical measures would destroy their creativity. Dressed in a suit and tie, and using language that belonged inside a corporate ingroup, I'd lost my audience before I'd even started.

Sue writes: Conversely, in my world, one individual showed up to a creative event wearing a suit and tie and was ridiculed – what was he wearing that for? Was he trying to look like he was in charge? And if so, why? Did he think he was better than everyone else, or was he going on to a job interview? He was treated with suspicion and excluded from any meaningful conversations.

These prejudicial reactions happen in situations where those with creative jobs interface with those who have non-creative jobs. This interface is becoming commonplace in many new industries and is becoming more important to legacy industries. Think about computer games companies such as Sony, advertising companies such as Bartle, Bogle & Hegarty, and travel companies such as Thomas Cook - creative work plays a fundamental and increasing role in defining their products and services. At a micro level the problem may be exposed by an artist being asked to create some computer game character designs free, or the accountant excluded from a design meeting. At a macro level, it's the designers who produce e-learning content and yet are expected to work in 19th century factory terms and conditions. On an individual level, when the lobotomy affects you, it can cause serious psychological harm.

Reconnecting

It is becoming increasingly important to understand the impact of the culturally-driven lobotomy, because in any programme of work, undervaluing a core skill creates a significant risk of failure. Imagine building a ship and ignoring the need to employ skilled designers and draughtsmen. This is a highly competitive world and no company or individual can afford to preserve a debilitating prejudice if they are to be successful. Creative skills are more important than ever; we need to value those skills and treat those who work in the creative industries with as much respect as we treat those who work in non-creative situations. Equally, creative entrepreneurs need to recognise their prejudice towards the world of more formal employment and work with the business sector to get their skills recognised, valued and included. For instance, the manufacture of an aeroplane requires skills in engineering and aviation science, but also there are the aesthetic design skills, marketing, web pages, graphics, colour schemes and fabric design. This represents the success of collaboration, which creates wealth and growth.

As an aside it is almost a paradox that those whose careers are based on their own creative skills are in effect business entrepreneurs (even though they might not see themselves in that way). To be successful they need to be as skilled at being an entrepreneur as they are at being a creator. Having a negative attitude to business methods (a commonplace response from the creative communities) is a philosophical contradiction.

We cannot afford to treat people differently on the basis of which workplace culture they prefer, the way they dress, speak or think. We cannot continue to value traditional skills and ignore those skills that lie at the heart of innovation and problem solving. We are in danger of creating a one-dimensional world, made up of measures and checks and balances, with little new at its centre. Policies aimed at prioritising narrow sciences above arts, and facts above new solutions, only serve to preserve the divide, and the prejudices that define its perimeters. How did the world's largest economy (the US), with the most resources, fall from 1st to 14th in the global rankings in terms of its educational achievements?[25] (Incidentally, the UK is now 20th) Part of the answer lies in the misguided value it places on people's ability to replicate rather than create.

Doing it differently

It's not just creativity that drives the new businesses; there is more value in the creative industries than just their raw talent. Organisations that have relied on stable systems and processes appropriate to an industrial age are in for a shock, as are individuals who expect a long-term career based on their academic degree results. Renowned strategy guru Gary Hamel warns in his book, *The Future of Management*[26], 'Your Company will be challenged to change in a way for which it has no precedent'. He argues that decades of orthodox decision-making practices by company management, and traditional organisational designs and approaches to employee relations, 'provide no real hope of avoiding painful restructurings'. Lowell Bryan and Claudia Joyce, two notable strategists with global business consultancy McKinsey & Co. agree. In their book, *Mobilizing Minds*[27], they arrive at a similar conclusion from a slightly different perspective. They find that the 20th century model of designing and managing companies, which emphasised hierarchy and the importance of labour and capital inputs, not only lags behind the need for companies today to encourage collaboration and wealth-creation by talented employees, but also actually generates unnecessary complexity that works at cross-purposes to those critical goals. Forward-looking executives will respond to this looming challenge, these authors conclude, by bringing the same energy to innovative management that they now bring to innovative products and services. Valuing talent, organising and reorganising creative teams quickly, being flexible, dedicated to the task, getting the job done, moving on - it all sounds familiar - in the creative work environment. There is a lot to learn from the way creative companies and individuals work, and it is they who are at the cutting edge, not the other way round.

Deep wounds

It's been played out over two centuries. Slowly, but surely, we've driven ourselves into a cul de sac, a dead end; but backing ourselves out of this will be fiercely resisted. This is because the decision makers and influential lobby groups: entrepreneurs, politicians, educationalists and academics are wedded to the lobotomy. For some it has been very beneficial; reputations have been built and fortunes made. Unpacking where it has taken root and exposing the sources that provide sustenance to its philosophies is where we turn next.

We may have got used to what the world has become, but it's time to reverse the perspective.

Part 2: Chapter 5: The cultural divide: Arts, science, education, business and sport

'Without culture, and the relative freedom it implies, society, even when perfect, is but a jungle. This is why any authentic creation is a gift to the future.'

- Albert Camus

'Without deviation from the norm, progress is not possible.'

- Frank Zappa

Taking root

How far has the lobotomy gone and how far has it spread? Has it become our way of life, infiltrating our policies and strategies, and becoming embedded within our economic, social and education systems? Has it become part of our modern culture?

Policy changes that have a negative effect on creative endeavour are underway in many countries, even if at first glance they appear to be focussed on kick-starting wealth creation through innovation and encouraging scientific research. There is no doubt that the gap between science and the humanities is widening as support for non-scientific activities is being withdrawn. We are not the first to voice concerns about the sharpening blades of cultural deforestation. The dangers of this for our future were explored by Stephen J Gould in his book *The Hedgehog, the Fox and The Magister's Pox (2003)*, which exposes the lie that 'science is the only true way forward' - a policy that favours one interest group over all others. Supporters of this 'single truth' are dramatised as foxes who use their elevated positions to claim that scientific knowledge alone can bring advancement. Gould examines the history of all forms of progress, and identifies creative thinking, the psychology of transcendence and discovery as the fundamental starting points. Without these there would be neither science nor art, which links directly to our point that the human mind must work holistically in order to bring improvements and new worthwhile developments; focussing on one capacity-rational thought - is not productive. In short, as science and the arts rely on the same human capacities, there is no reason to exclude or favour any one skill over another. The arguments are really a smokescreen that serves to promote the interests of the science community over all other groups.

In education, the emphasis is now on rote learning, tethered to a reward system based on memory and eschewing unique thought. This plays to a desperate strategy - copying the past in the vain hope that a new future will emerge. Added to this is a new financial burden designed to motivate students to work hard - the student loan. Apparently in many western countries we can no longer afford to pay to educate our young people; student debt in the US now runs into trillions of dollars. Similar levels of debt are piling up in the UK. The student loan system is an accountancy solution; it ignores the psychological and motivational impact on students and educators and does not consider the risks of damaging longer term economic outcomes. Students are now shackled to huge debts, and so aim for standard well paid *existing* careers to minimise financial risk. Of course it is then only a short step to coerce students to take courses with more certainty of a job at the end; the employability card is being played. Such guarantees are much harder to make for innovative industries, and non-technical courses. Arts-based courses and colleges specialising in creative subjects are closing due to dwindling resources, as students find that funding criteria, parental pressure and government policy all channel them towards a science-based or technical education. What remains of the arts provision is increasingly favouring digital media courses, which are tightly managed and delivered by colleges specialising in technical subjects, ensuring the students think and present evidence in a logical and scientific manner.

With funding for arts and non-profit sectors being squeezed as a consequence of the recent global economic downturn - itself partly caused by our dehumanising direction - private philanthropists are being encouraged to provide the short-fall in funding. It won't be the large established arts organisations that will suffer, as they can attract wealthy sponsors through their brand relationship with 'high quality' arts. It is the small local arts organisations who are likely to find things much harder. One of the principles of state arts funding, that it should address local as well as national provision, will inevitably disappear. Crowd funding through internet sites such as Kickstarter hold much promise and may well end up as the route of choice to fund many creative projects and even start-up businesses. It is early days but one thing is clear - new market forces will change the way both sides approach commercial opportunities.

Business change – markets, buyers and sellers

But is this a good thing? Could it be seen as a return to commercial realism for the creative community? And what is the creative community anyway? We already know that the extremes (boxes and diamonds) of any divide can become stereotypes that engender prejudice. In our view the creative work place and the more orthodox work place are in reality just the opposite ends of a continuum, and creativity will be deployed all along this continuum in various ways, hence we can talk about creative solutions within every discipline, involving people acting creatively in financial services as well as computer games development or within advertising campaigns.

In his book *Managing Creativity* Chris Bilton explains that the marketplace for creative products operates very differently from the marketplace for conventional goods:

Creative marketplaces have a loose arrangement of many small independent creators and craftspeople constantly developing new ideas at the perimeter, which is a large and busy place. Meetings are often arranged in social settings around an event (or the pub) and the agenda is open. At its core lie a few corporations that forage within this marketplace to find new ideas that they can then sell on a larger scale; traditionally this model would fit the market for books, music or art. Publishers seek out new authors and if they think their ideas will sell in the wider marketplace they will offer a publishing deal. Some may become very successful, but the majority achieve only moderate or no success. There are few barriers to entry, new ideas occur regularly and every product needs to be unique in some way (even if it's derived from existing work). Copyright law makes this market viable, offering protection from illegal copying and product piracy. Contrast this with conventional markets, which tend to be dominated by a core of large corporations that employ vast numbers of people. These companies make up the majority of the players in the market and have many tightly managed rules and regulations, inherited from their 'Taylorist' beginnings. In this model, finding space for new ideas and innovation is a challenge, so making small incremental improvements to existing processes and products is often much easier and the norm. Examples of incremental creativity or innovation are products such as the computer operating system MS/Windows with its continuous development of new versions, and the word processing system MS/Word, the latest version of which is being used to capture the ideas in this book. In these markets the core is an industrious place; meetings in offices are arranged in advance, agendas laid and attendees notified. These markets are huge, and diversity of products is encouraged by open competition. The strength of any players is determined by their market share, and the control they exert can prevent others from entering the market.[28] The perimeter is much thinner, made up of smaller companies who are often tightly bound to the larger players. Bilton proposes that the creative marketplace can be managed but in different ways from the standard approach. Policies that encourage 'drop-by networking' and unstructured meetings are likely to encourage growth and collaboration in contrast to the highly structured and formal conference based approach of conventional markets.

However the internet is changing these models. Over 5% of books published in the UK in 2013 were self-published – a growth rate of around 80% year on year (source *Neilson book scan*). Amazon, Lulu and other internet businesses now offer systems that remove the need for a 'legacy' publisher, and companies such as CDBaby offer similar services for musicians. To use these services effectively the creators need to take on the tasks previously provided by the record labels and publishers: marketing product development and financial management. In effect the creators become the managers of their creative business, a task that many find daunting and often draining. They also need to deal with quality issues, such as book jacket design and layout as well as copy editing.

In theory this independent approach provides the mechanism to sell directly to customers, increasing the diversity of products available and providing the creators with a larger share of the income generated. Previously a record deal or a book publishing deal would be a prerequisite to entry into the market. Today the barriers to entry are being removed, the costs of reproduction are almost zero, and distribution can be achieved instantaneously. For many aggregators this is causing transformational change, but for creators the new marketplace is an opportunity, provided they can manage their business successfully.

In his book *The Long Tail: Why the Future of Business Is Selling Less of More,* Chris Anderson[29] challenges the status quo. His view is that new modern market conditions, enabled by information technology and the Internet, mean it is possible to sell many more unique products that otherwise may have been uneconomic to produce. This particularly applies to products that can be replicated easily for little cost – for example e-books and digital music. Many more artists have access to the market, and the gatekeeper role as traditionally practised by record companies and publishers is being eroded by organisations employing the new strategy, such as Amazon (mentioned above). Major record companies have seen their conventional market shrink dramatically; since 2001 in the USA market for recorded music has dropped from 16 to 8 billion dollars[30]. These figures do not include the rise of independent music (which now accounts for 35% of the market in the US and 24% in the UK). If you are a creative musician, being business-savvy in these conditions is one of the most important skills to develop. Managing your own career is a viable way forward, rather than signing over your rights to a record label.

The opportunity is here today. Taking advantage of it is another matter. Attitudes that hinder success, such as claiming that the business tasks would damage creativity, or that the tasks are too complicated, drive artists back towards the old models. Success in these new markets depends being an entrepreneur – albeit a creative one.

The picture is one of an economic world where creative entrepreneurs are isolated from formal business skills and processes, divided by behaviours, expectations, work-culture, attitudes and rewards. In contrast formal business struggles to innovate, has little understanding of creativity and segregates itself inside unwieldy in-group structures that are impenetrable to outsiders. It may have developed this way for good reasons. But if it works so well, why are we in danger of failing? What is the big worry?

The innovation crisis

It's a catchy phrase, but what does it mean? If like many you take the number of patent registrations as a measure of how innovative we are then the most recent data should put your mind at ease. According to the World Intellectual Property Organisation[31] IP filing activity for 2012 shows that patent filings grew by 9.2 % year on year – the fastest growth over the past 18 years. Similarly, industrial design counts grew by 17 % – the fastest growth on record. Trademark class counts saw healthy growth of 6.0 %, although below the 2010 and 2011 growth rates. While this may appear globally positive these figures hide marked differences in IP filing trends across different parts of the world. China – the recipient of most patent, trademark, and industrial design filings – is the principal force behind the increase in global IP-filing, whereas European registrations stagnated. (The US and Korea remain largely flat). The question is what are these patents? China is experiencing a catch-up growth spurt, which has led to the world's worst city pollution estimated to be the equivalent of smoking 40 cigarettes per day. Are the patents to solve issues like this or patents to make more of what we already have?

Recently Bruce Nussbaum, the author of the book *Creative Intelligence*[32] provided his own take on the state of policy innovation and education in the US. Sparked by findings that showed only a tiny percentage of US business now do any R&D[33], his book details the sorry state of our wealth generating system, a system that was once made up of many diverse opportunities for investment and growth. Think of railroads, engineering, computers, electricity, clothing, automobiles - the list goes on. It turns out that one of the many problems leading to what is being termed the 'innovation crisis' is that over the last 20 years much of government and industry funding has been channelled into just one technology: bioscience. This was because it was sold as the next big thing to follow the digital revolution, and potentially be just as lucrative. But bioscience hasn't delivered the expected new products that would extend life, deal with disease and illness, and enable the manufacture of organ replacements – and despite a fresh round of hype these futuristic products are nowhere to be seen. So Nussbaum's recommendations are to dismantle this focus and restart the creativity that once brought us success. That means stopping funding just one technology and restarting the 'making culture' of manufacturing. To support this he advocates changing the education system: moving away from 'teaching to the test' and putting people in government who are not part of Wall Street. The intention would be to eliminate student debt and introduce training for creativity. In his view today we don't even know what the urgent problems are because we are so focused on the past, and memory tests. How can we move forward when we don't even know what we're supposed to be solving?

This view is supported by former world chess champion Garry Kasparov and Paypal founder Peter Thiel. In an article published in the *Financial Times* they argue that the collapse in world economic growth is due to stagnation in technology and innovation[34]. Economist Robert Gordon also suggests that today's technological innovations are much less significant than breakthroughs such as electricity, clean water and the internal combustion engine[35]. This impacts negatively on wealth creation, i.e. there is nothing worth investing in, and explains why we seem to be facing a century of stagnation and debt.

You may think that we are pressing forward with computers and communications, and that our world is ultra modern, but in reality most of the computer technology we see and use today was devised in the 1970s. The sheen that makes us think we live in an ultra modern world with iPads, smart phones and social media platforms is made up of computer software programmes and hardware that were invented almost 50 years ago. Reinvention is the term used when an existing technology is upgraded and sold as something new. Which version of MS/Windows or Apple OS are you using? Silicon Valley, the 'hotbed of innovation', could be more accurately known as the 'hotbed of re-invention'. Add to this the focus on patent infringement[36] and a dim picture emerges; one where corporations are struggling to find anything new to sell. Maybe this wouldn't matter if we didn't need new ideas, but we do. We have global problems and they won't go away on their own.

Testing testing one two testing

We've probably all done an IQ test at some point in our lives. In the US the Torrance test is similar, but instead of just measuring the intelligence quotient (IQ), the test also measures creativity. It is largely based on measuring divergent thinking - an example question might be: 'Here's a sponge, what else could you do with it other than mop up water?' The aim is to come up with as many novel uses for the sponge as possible in a limited timeframe. The next step is to measure convergent thinking - that is the ability to sift ideas and pick the best. Since the 1950s this test has been taken by millions of children in the USA. It has always shown an increase in both creativity and IQ, tracking a rise in affluence and access to education. However, recent analysis shows an alarming trend; since 1990, creativity has *fallen* year by year, it is among the youngest children that the trend is most marked - those that should have a natural ability for divergent thinking.

This evidence suggests we have a looming creativity crisis, compounding our cycle of dwindling innovation. Will we ever be able to recover?

Indestructible creativity

Even in the gulags of soviet Russia, Aleksandr Solzhenitsyn found the inspiration and energy to write[37]. Louis Pasteur was prompted to discover treatments for disease following the deaths of three of his five children from typhoid. You have to try very hard to crush creativity, but unfortunately our modern education systems attempt to do exactly that.

As Ken Robinson points out in his book *Out Of Our Minds*[38] - and in his amusing but starkly challenging presentation, *Changing Education Paradigms*[39], - young children are masters of divergent thinking, which is a hallmark of creative ability. We are all born with this ability, we can all do it, and we enjoy it. Give these children a problem that requires new ideas or uses of every day objects and they excel; 98% of kindergarten children scored 'genius' level in tests designed to assess divergent thinking ability, but by the age of 14 those same children have largely lost this talent – it has deteriorated during the intervening years in which they have become 'educated'[40]. The so-called 'progressive age' has applied the principles of scientific management to education (as well as to economics, politics, governance, business and finance). This broadened access to education, but the type of education offered was based on an academic v non-academic view of the world. While this may have been a suitable starting position, unfortunately it is where it has stayed. Without modernising the needs of education, the engine of scientific management has refined its processes in line with 'Taylorist' thinking: standardised testing with exams set and marked by computers, schools organised along factory lines such as set timetables, separate subjects, ringing bells, lunch breaks, performance indicators, year on year improvement and batch processing of year groups. It's all about standardisation, but as any parent will tell you their children are anything but standard - they have unique skills, preferences, abilities and personalities. In our production line education system conformity is rewarded, diversity is not.

Diversity is an important component of evolution because homogeneity and standardisation will inevitably lead to an atrophy of new ideas (not to mention the gene pool). The fundamental principles of capitalist economic growth: collaboration, innovation, investment and development, are undermined without diversity. The sort of problems we can expect to see are flat or negative growth in developed economies that have hit a ceiling of creativity. Expect to see more high value products being made cheaply in developing nations, investment in undesirable or intangible goods and services, more financial fraud, a preference for low risk options, short-termism, high levels of unemployment, western economies shrinking, unsolved global problems, a famine of innovation, increasing divide between rich and poor, a shortage of resources leading to social and political unrest. Does this sound familiar? Economies need maintenance and development. As more is developed more must be maintained. It is all too easy to take the low risk option, a maintenance-based economy, which eventually will be unable to sustain future generations.

One aspect of contemporary education that deserves further exploration is multiple choice questions and testing. The aim of scientific management is to relentlessly improve efficiency and productivity, and standardisation and automation are used extensively in industrial settings to achieve this. Likewise, this education model must test constantly to ensure targets are being met and standards maintained. If the aim is to test in the most efficient way, then ticking the correct box or using exactly the right phrasing or vocabulary is easier to assess, aggregate and report on than reading unique individual scripts. The time saved is significant, and machines can be employed to scan and interpret results quickly and easily. Children are trained to deal with such tests, then the results are used to rank schools, which have little option but to follow the herd. (Sue writes: Once, when I was working in a small creative college, the staff were asked to complete an elementary test in English and Mathematics, the same one the students were taking. Despite holding high level qualifications in these subjects, many of the staff failed the test because they did not answer using language that the computer programme understood or expected, so even though the answers were correct they were marked wrong). However, real world problems are rarely presented in this way. Imagine being asked to come up with some new ideas for city transport systems, and being told to choose one of three answers; it is hardly the future of commerce and business. Where are the new ideas and products coming from if the next generation think the world's problems can be boiled down to one of three answers, and the correct one is at the back, printed upside down, or only available once the exam is no longer live?

But when did education provide for creativity? Isn't education what it always was – a system of knowledge transfer from generation to generation, managed through factual learning, tests, assessments and awards? When was it anything else? Perhaps it is the success or mechanisation of the process that has led to the doubts. Perhaps education's DNA can't change, it's just got too efficient at it and is now excluding divergence and diversity through a more determined system, one that is designed to achieve memory-based results. Perhaps our education systems are now actively discouraging creativity, whereas in the past they were tolerant and agnostic if not promotional. Other reasons such as cultural change must also have an impact. Is there enough time for creativity in our lives – remember creativity needs time, and if you introduce the Internet, social networking, 200 channel TV, both parents at work, an ipod and a mobile phone, where has the time gone for creativity development – a development that needs to take place everywhere – not just in a school room?

Today we hear much in the media about the dumbing down of education, of a growing divide between educational opportunities for rich and poor, declining pupil achievement, the use of calming drugs to deal with hyperactivity. We hear business complaints about the capabilities of school leavers and graduates, motivational issues and general behaviour issues of our young people. It is likely that we are experiencing the consequences of manufacturing an education system for machines not humans.

Understanding creativity

Creativity - and those who are engaged with it - has been the subject of many academic studies and is a subject found in multiple disciplines. Psychology, sociology, philosophy and neuroscience have published research that attempts to understand creativity from a particular viewpoint. The differences between those who work creatively and those who don't, and the environments that promote creativity, offer fascinating areas for research. Two of the best-known researchers in this field are Mihaly Csikszentmihalyi [41] (author of the bestselling book, *Flow: The Psychology Of Optimal Experience*) and Teresa Amabile[42], who has studied creative environments, identifying 'algorithmic learning' as a negative feature of our modern education systems.

Csikszentmihalyi proposes a direct link between reaching a state of creative competency underlined by a life of study and practice, and true happiness. Interviewing four hundred high achieving creators from all walks of life, his conclusion is that they reach a unique state that allows them to be immensely creative within their discipline. Their discipline can be in the arts, science, business, entertainment or sports (in fact any area is appropriate). This state he calls FLOW. The state of flow can only be entered once total control has been learnt through a high level of skill and arousal stimulated by difficult challenges. Also of interest are the states of boredom and apathy, which are a consequence of low skills and low challenges. In short, happiness cannot be achieved without hard work in both dimensions.

However, there needs to be a growth factor applied to such a model. For example it is clearly possible for a very young person to be in a state of flow (immersed in a creative task); it doesn't depend on being a recognised genius. To maintain the potential for flow, skills need to be continuously improved through learning, while the new knowledge is formed into thinking capacity through the solving of challenges. These challenges allow discovery to take place (risk-taking). There is an implied balance within the flow model. Both creative and logical skills are required to produce valuable outcomes. Sadly there are many graduates doing menial work who know the emotional impact of imbalance; boredom - highly skilled, but lightly challenged.

Living the nightmare

Below we present some facts and figures and recent interviews that support the view that creative skills are being relentlessly devalued in everyday life.

We interviewed Mary, who is a good photographer. Her portfolio is vast, but she's been trying to make a living for many years. She told us that she often gets proposals in which a magazine will ring her to ask if they could use one of her photos. They then go on to say that there is no fee, but they would put a link to her web site in the magazine. In many cases Mary would give in and agree. They'll use her photo, but invariably she will get no consequential work and no money. Mary is usually broke.

In contrast Matt is a good plumber. He was asked to quote for a job to replace some old lead pipe, install a new radiator and a shower unit. He gave the client the quote. He carried out the work. He got paid.

In 2010 there were 1,563 vacancies for computer games designers (requiring skills in both art and maths) in the UK. There were 13 applicants. (*Source NESTA report*)[43].

In 2012, a year starting with high levels of unemployment in Europe and the US, heading up the list of the top 100 companies to work for in the US was software giant SAS, closely followed by Boston Consulting and Google. These 100 companies had 17,000+ vacancies between them. They want people who can solve problems and think outside the box[44].

Three to four percent of the world's children are diagnosed with attention deficit hyperactivity disorder (ADHD). Most of these children live in the US and the most common medication used to treat them is Ritalin. They display behaviours that suggest they do not concentrate sufficiently to make progress at school. ADHD has spread to the UK and other western countries[45].

In 2013, 2.49 million people were unemployed in the UK. Of these 1.02 million were 16-24 year olds who were not in education, employment or training (NEET).

It's not that bad is it?

Stagnation is a term used by economists to describe zero growth. The term is used in science and broadly means 'when things stop moving' - like stagnant water in a pond. Try standing still for an hour - how does it feel? With a lot of effort you might make it through a few minutes but not much more. When we run out of ideas, when we spend our time on worthless activities, or produce 'me too' products, (for example there are over one hundred different products all made from aspirin) and then pretend there will always be a miracle around the corner. That's getting close to economic stagnation. We have a history of trying to convince ourselves that there is always a new idea somewhere. In 1999 it was the 'tiger' economy of Ireland[46], then Iceland, then the countries of Eastern Europe. These economies experienced rapid economic growth and a rise in living standards much like China today. In most cases this was followed by stagnation. Today the new tiger, we are often told, is the 'creative industries'.

Richard Florida in his book *'The Rise of the Creative Class'*[47] provides an analysis of this new group. Smart, hip and wealthy, they are the programmers, designers and artists of the new information age. However, whilst it may well be a good idea to look at the new successful class based on the computer industry, lumping them together with the creative community simply means that the true condition of those who work as creatives is masked by an ocean of new IT industry success. Certainly, this new class is leading the way in terms of respect, reward, status, self-esteem and success, but the reality is that the people who work in the creative community are treated like second class citizens every day, every week, every year. Whether it's a 360 music record deal (where the management not only take a cut of all your music sales, but also of all your live performances and merchandising), a 3% book deal, pirated copies of films, music, software and video games, illegal use of copyrights, investors who walk away because they don't understand or education policies that insist on fact regurgitation in order to pass exams, the creatives are being shredded. The real tiger is still trying to get out of its cage, a cage built by 19th century corporate culture. In a world where governments are run by lobbyists and banks run like casinos, everywhere the creative industries turn leads to a road seemingly patrolled by thieves and vagabonds. Add to this the stuck mindset of an industrial revolution that happened 250 years ago, oversized bureaucracies, obscene income inequalities, the madness of 'one size fits all' - but easy-to-measure - education policies, and you get a clear picture of what's got to change.

The new digital age has encouraged a rethink of working methods: how we as humans collaborate and interact to create what we need. There is a coming revolution in working practice and it includes many creative industries, either because they decided to do it that way deliberately, or because it happened organically - it was the best way to do modern stuff. Visit any of the new giant IT companies: Apple, Microsoft, Google or the production houses that create digitally enhanced movies - they are all embracing the change, one that demands that their workforces are both creative and businesslike, in short, human.

The new revolution is waiting to take on the future, but it means we have to change our ways. After all, the industrial revolution started in a few industries and spread quickly through market forces, just as the new revolution is doing. A recent study by Forrester Research[48] found that companies that embrace creativity outperform peers and competitors on many aspects of success, including revenue growth, market share, and talent acquisition. Quoting from the report: *'They enjoy a high-performance working environment, driven by progressive leaders and managers who provide processes, methods, and funding to back creative initiatives'*. Working the creative way is fast becoming the new normal, so we need to get used to it; 9-5 lifelong careers may soon no longer exist, there is no need to dress up in blue or grey suits anymore, or to formalise everything into a one hour meeting on a Monday morning. On the other side of the fence, burying your head in a creative sandpit won't cut the mustard either.

The consequences of the lobotomy mean we don't get along or collaborate effectively anymore. We either don't value creative activity or we think business is for stuffed shirts, and we don't take people seriously who aren't like us. We either think the way forward is to go back to the industrial age, or to lose ourselves in our creative world, bumble along and hope the 'real' one goes away. This just doesn't work; it never has, and it never will.

On your marks... get set...

Why does this divide between our creative and logical minds, and the prejudice that it engenders, not affect sport in the same way? There may be egos and hubris, but not because the fans think their heroes or heroines have sold out when they accept sponsorship and advertising deals, or because the sportsmen and women think commercialism would undo their purity. Sponsorship is natural, as is advertising and endorsement. Isn't sport, in many ways, a perfect example of the use of all our talents, creativity and logic, working together with a finely honed sense of control and planning? In answer, the history of sport is very different from that of creativity and the arts. In some sports such as football, baseball, rugby and cricket it has developed from a pastime into big business. However, the holistic essence of human achievement is embraced, not rejected or isolated. To succeed competitors must use every skill that a person can possess. Imagine being told success depends on dropping your imaginative, creative mindset and adopting a purely logical repetitive approach to any sport. In the film 'Zidane'[49] the soccer star is portrayed thinking deeply about the strategies during the game, imagining how play would pan out based on his research, his knowledge and his emotions. All of his talents are at work to create the outcome he wants.

In the book *Outliers*[50] Malcolm Gladwell references a rule of thumb for success in any walk of life - an indicator developed by K. Anders Ericsson - which is that at least 10,000 hours of practice is needed to become an expert in any field. This can equally be applied to Olympic gold medallist Usain Bolt, entrepreneur Sir Richard Branson or the pop singer Lady Ga Ga. Whether you agree with his proposition or not there is a clear link between creativity and rationality thereby using all human abilities and the achievement of success.

The lobotomy had to focus on activities that would undermine the new zeitgeist. It had to encourage support for logical and rational behaviour and thinking, then demote and reduce creativity and emotional thinking as far as possible to ensure success of a machine-driven world. Sport was neutral and at the time underdeveloped as a business sector; sport has human achievement at the top of its priorities; sport needs creativity and emotion linked to rationality and logic.

Today interest in the creative thinking aspects of sport has begun to take the main stage in the search for better performances once the processing of what is known, which becomes part of the subconscious, has been exhausted. Complex competitive strategies and powerful imagined successful outcomes all contribute to sporting success, particularly in team sports. The word creative is accepted and used within sport; there is no baggage. When discussing a creative play or strategy no-one suggests it be called invention or innovation, as happens in science and business, so there is no conflict. Sports coaches are clear about what the mind needs to achieve. Once that has been discovered through training they can implement and integrate it, and succeed.

Whatever path people may choose for their lives, whether it be sport, science, business or the arts, it is clear that the role played by creativity is fundamental to success. Our creativity must be supported by our logical rational skills and a natural balance maintained. In sports that is accepted and understood, but in the arts, business and science some repair work is needed. At a national level policy must be altered and our state run systems that we trust to develop our young people must be recast; we must all call for change and we need to start soon.

Part 2: Chapter 6: Why now?

'Fear stifles our thinking and actions. It creates indecisiveness that results in stagnation. I have known talented people who procrastinate indefinitely rather than risk failure. Lost opportunities cause erosion of confidence, and the downward spiral begins.'

- Charles Stanley

Success

The inexorable rise of the production line, the creation of wealth associated with high-volume, low-cost products and the division of high-value skilled labour into low-value repeatable, and ultimately automatable, machine-driven tasks, has been a huge success. That success has seen products such as cars and washing machines, televisions and computers brought within the reach of many consumers, whilst driving up the living standards of millions of people.

However, the arts and crafts sector has suffered as the value of their activities has become disconnected from the new mainstream economics, so replacement funding models have been developed. Part of the aim is to keep alive the skills and lifestyles that have begun to represent a cultural value, ostensibly becoming a mark of modern civilisation, and attracting altruistic and sympathetic support from governments and private philanthropists. More recently this approach has included large numbers of small donations made through crowd-funding web sites. This larger scale funding model is also applied to the general non-profit sector (charities) and voluntary organisations. It often takes the form of grants, bursaries, gifts (bequests) and so on. This funding may be provided by government organisations (Arts Council England, for example) or through trusts such as The Sainsbury Family Charitable Trust, who in turn may be funded by philanthropic individuals or private companies, or organisations such as the Heritage Lottery Fund in the UK.

This works so long as we accept that the products which creative communities produce, both tangible and intangible, are outside the mainstream and can't be valued or used in the same way as consumer products. It also has to be agreed that funding such products is morally correct, and that to live like this is socially acceptable and economically sustainable. It begins to atrophy as a viable way of living if these principles are withdrawn. So, if the altruistic value attached to creative work declines, the reason to support it is weakened. If the creators become aloof or elitist, it becomes far more difficult to justify tax-based or charitable funding, and if the economic or social value of this type of creative work reduces, then other more commercially or socially productive avenues will have to be sought. In this environment, creative activity will be vulnerable to economic downturns. Occupying a low priority in the pecking order of economic activity means that when things get tough, creatives are likely to be the first to lose out. Hence 'justifying the arts' is an energy-sapping activity which occurs with monotonous regularity throughout economic cycles.

The value of art

The devaluing of creativity and the isolation of the arts and crafts from mainstream economics led to a change in definition in the West. In the field of science, the word 'creativity' disappeared from the lexicon. Creativity became associated purely with the arts - science and business apparently did not need it any longer. Terms like 'creative accountancy' became pejorative business speak for inaccurate, unreliable and untrustworthy practises. Innovation - seen to be a more measurable process as opposed to creativity (a capability) - became the subject of study and investment. Creativity instead became a focus for psychologists, not economists or educationalists. Activities that were related to our natural long-term imaginations and creativity were downgraded, while those associated with our short-term administration were upgraded. To be successful was the product of hard work - long hours spent learning facts, and the element of creativity involved in discovery was sidelined. The consequences would take a long time to impact, generations would slip by, arguably the periods of greatest need during the world wars would demand the return of our ingenuity and creativity, and then were rapidly forgotten once the benefits were harvested.

In his *Dimbleby Lecture* on BBC (28 Feb 2012)[51] leading geneticist and Nobel laureate Sir Paul Nurse made an impassioned plea for a bigger role for science, emphasising the need for more science in schools in particular. As he pointed out, science, together with politics and commerce, leads to wealth generating innovation. He used the Lunar Society[52] (the influential group of free thinkers referred to in chapter 4) as an example of this laudable collaborative culture. Curiously, he used the word creativity just once in an hour-long lecture. While his focus was on more funding for science and for more science in the curriculum, he did not recognise the key role of creativity within that objective, perhaps because that word is now attached to the arts. Within the academic community, the words 'innovation' and 'invention' generally refer to the latter stages of the creative process - the parts that are easiest to measure and formulate into systemic processes, when the 'product' begins to emerge, but there is a lot that goes on before that happens. To once again quote Albert Einstein; *Not everything that is of value can be measured, and not everything that can be measured has value.*

In the US, the UK, mainland Europe and many other westernised countries, economic catastrophe has been stalking governments and businesses since 2008. Predictions vary but some pundits see years of austerity ahead. *Money Week*, a specialist UK publication aimed at providing advice to professional investors, predicts just such a situation. Local councils in the UK have been drawing up 'graphs of doom' to illustrate the sorry state they predict they will be in, in the not too distant future. The *Financial Times* is less pessimistic, as is the *Wall Street Journal*, but they both portray a bleaker future based on similar indicators and outlooks. This has prompted a global cutback in government spending, which some view as a loss of nerve. In the UK, a coalition government was elected in May 2010 on a platform of spending cuts and the introduction of a new way of contributing to a collaborative and magnanimous 'Big Society'. A government proposal contained within a pre-legislative white paper entitled 'Giving' (May 2011)[53] was intended to pave the way to increase private donations and volunteering, whilst reducing government support in the non-profit and arts sectors. The 'public sector social value act' was passed in 2012 stating that when choosing suppliers, public sector bodies must in future look at social as well as financial value.

But will these policies designed to support the arts and other not-for-profit enterprises by encouraging philanthropy actually work? In his book, *Bowling Alone* (2000), Robert Putman draws a distinction between two types of philanthropy: that which contributes to social capital, and that which doesn't. 'Doing with'- that is, making social connections as part of the activity does make a difference, 'doing for' does not. If you want to improve society, simply getting more people to give is unlikely to work. Putman's book attempts to find the underlying causes of American society's dismemberment. A closely knit community full of popular local clubs, such as ten pin bowling clubs, is reduced to fear-ridden isolation - bowling alone - over a period of 50 years, why? His primary answer points to the rise of television and the demise of the church as a social network hub for local communities. Industrialisation and the growth of the cities initially took with it the cultures of agrarian communities, forged into new city networks. But these, he maintains, were eventually undermined by changes in the communication industries, providing an example of how change can take place right under your nose, every day, every year, until the damage becomes palpable and almost irreparable.

At the same time, almost all western governments are reviewing educational qualifications with a view to re-calibrating subjects, so that 'hard' subjects such as maths and economics attract greater value than relatively 'easy' subjects (arts and literature, social sciences). There is also a new 'employability' policy that measures the success of higher education institutions in terms of the numbers of graduates that find paid employment. Self-employment, which is the destination of many creatives, does not 'count' and therefore these careers often disappear from the statistics, thus making creative graduates look less successful. This will inevitably lead to a concentration of subjects and courses towards those disciplines that lead to stronger conventional employment prospects and the removal of courses that are associated with weaker less measurable marketplaces. However no-one can predict the long-term strength of markets in terms of employability; many of today's industries may not exist in 20 years time: was there a job called web designer 20 years ago? Or SEO consultant? (search engine optimisation). This policy aimed at reducing creative activity seems to fly in the face of economic trends. If Richard Florida is right, the creative class need to be widely read and numerate, as well as creative.

Clearly the world and its values are being challenged by these pressures to comply. The relentless re-adoption of historical methods of working in an attempt to re-create the economic growth associated with industrialisation is still shackled to the same logic that would propose introducing horse drawn transport as a solution to car congestion.

Unequal advantage

The impact of this type of leadership is inevitably destructive, leading to job cuts, high levels of long term youth unemployment, conversion of jobs into modern day slavery via unpaid internships, the re-introduction of trade apprenticeships to solve the 'unemployable' claims, a widening wealth gap, and social unrest as the 'haves' and 'have-nots' become polarised. In effect, a return to 19th century inequalities.

The success of industrialisation was a combination of creativity and the development of innovative processes, together with a rising sense of equality and egalitarianism. Our future relies on the same combination, a balance of wealth-generating activities and respect for our talents and ambitions.

In the book *The Spirit Level* by Richard Wilkinson and Kate Pickett (first published in March 2009, about six months after the start of the financial crisis of 2008) they place much of the blame for the current financial meltdown on risks taken by people in the financial sector 'whose excesses were matched only by their grotesquely inflated salaries'. The authors amass considerable compelling evidence that we have a strong innate sense of equality, which is being corrupted and ignored, and that tipping points have occurred previously when similar historical imbalances have appeared that led to catastrophic events. They point out that despite regulation there are few checks and balances in developed countries to control greed and corruption. They paint a picture of political and economic dishonesty that feels all too familiar. In these circumstances, funding sources are going to get tougher to find, and tougher to convince.

How should the creative community respond? What's coming down the line?

In their *Harvard Business Review* article, *How to Give Away Money More Effectively* Robert Kaplan and Alan Grossman[54] outline how the same measures and metrics that have been applied to the commercial sector should be developed for the non-profit sector. This broadly means adopting many of the operational management systems that the creative sector despises. This approach sets up a constant improvement cycle, where performance indicators are calculated that allow comparisons of all competing organisations (competition is, of course, no stranger to the creative sector). The results are used to help make decisions about where to place funding so that whatever the funder wants to achieve will be delivered in the most cost effective way. This would impact non-government organisations (NGOs): groups that do charity work, without financial support of the government - for example, *Doctors Without Borders*[55]. They point out that many of the social problems they seek to fix are large scale, like inner-city poverty. These large-scale solutions require large-scale organisation. The piecemeal nature of the NGO sector, coupled with a lack of accountability, mitigates against effective change and improvement. The future, they claim, must be about the growth of the best, whilst investing in promising ideas that fit with a range of social problems that can be addressed by innovative solutions. Muddling along from grant-to-grant, year-by-year and spending money ineffectively will not cut it in the future. The focus here is on the charitable sector, but the funding principles can equally be applied to the arts.

An example of a progressive funding organisation is the Robin Hood Foundation in New York City[56]. They filter donations to those organisations that prove that they can deliver their main aim - to raise the income levels of the poor in the city. Another organisation, United Way, provide the largest source of funding for this kind of purpose in the USA, they too have changed their approach, now demanding that all of their client organisations demonstrate community benefits from the work they do, something that has upset many traditional NGOs. The business of business is coming.

To take advantage of this change, those on the receiving end need to 'up' their business savvy and know how. This means getting to grips with business measures, collecting performance information, presenting business cases and organising for the long term. Ultimately, it should provide a far more stable environment for

NGOs and prove more beneficial for their clients. In terms of non-commercial activities in the creative sector similar disciplines may soon be imposed.

Funding of commercial creative enterprise is also due for a shake up, but for different reasons. The capital markets are readily available to all forms of traditional business: venture capital funds, banks and business angels provide funding for business start-up and growth. Creative sector businesses have a much more difficult time raising finance and gaining support from governments[57]. Overall UK business has suffered a considerable downturn in R&D and innovation since 2008[58].

To supplement the lack of capital investors, it is traditional for a large player within a creative sector to act as banker, providing investment funds (advances) offset against returns. Film studios have maintained this role for many years, as have record companies and book publishers. With the fragmentation of these markets and the arrival of the Internet, new dynamics are set to open up these markets as never before - to those who are aware and ready to take advantage. iTunes was introduced by Apple on January 9, 2001. On February 24, 2010, Apple announced that over 10 billion tracks had been downloaded from the iTunes store. It is now the biggest retailer of digital music in the world, controlling over 80% of the market. Companies like Spotify are competing to repeat this success for streaming music services. Recording artists too can develop their own career without the use of record companies. Independent films can gain a worldwide audience, if the content has strong viral-ability. Films can be viewed in the home over the internet, pop-up cinemas can be set up quickly and easily. Digital distribution has eliminated the costs of film printing. Books can be published through Amazon or Lulu with no legacy publisher involved, thousands of books can be stored and read on a device weighing less than a kilogram. Internet services provide ways of living that have never existed before: Facebook, Instagram, Twitter, LinkedIn, Google and a myriad of networking opportunities yet to come to share and communicate via hand-held devices, portable computers and desktops. The traditional ways of thinking, acting and behaving in these creative markets is becoming obsolete.

Creative management

Paradoxically it is within the creative sector, in particularly media and technology companies, where much of the leading edge progress has taken place. The expertise is also bleeding across into traditional business: online retailing, banking, leisure and so on. Hence a slew of new jobs have appeared: web designers, web masters, security experts, digital graphic designers, SEO managers, content producers, content authors, games designers and e-learning experts. Combining these skills with new information technologies has provided a launch pad for a revolution in marketing and sales. In this new world product endorsement is no longer a dirty word and we are beginning to see up-and-coming bands modelling branded designer shirts whilst still maintaining their 'street cred'.

The picture that emerges is one of vast change. Now, more than ever, the two apparently incompatible sectors are poised to develop entirely new ways of managing and conducting business. Among the many barriers to change are memes ('inheritable' social genes) developed for a different age. Clinging on the beliefs that somehow creative activity is separated from the mainstream, that people involved in it must be isolated, are the hallmarks of a bygone age. Today, we all need each other.

At Ferrari the culture of creativity is actively encouraged. In a *Harvard Business Review* article, director of human resources and organisation, Mario Almondo, was asked how Ferrari trains its employees to be creative, to which he responded:

'You can't methodically teach creativity. But you can provide an environment that nurtures it. Several times a year, we run a programme called Creativity Club that is designed to get employees' creative juices flowing. We have six events at which employees meet various types of artists. We've had painters, sculptors, a jazz musician, a writer, a radio DJ, a photographer, a chef, an actor, an orchestra conductor, and others. The goal is for our employees to learn about how artists generate ideas and solutions.'

Ferrari isn't the only company that cares about the personal growth of its employees. At Pixar University, 110 courses on everything from improvisation to self defence are taught to all employees. The point of this in-house education is to 'push Pixar employees to try new things, work together better and test new ideas.'

In his book, *Innovate the Pixar Way*, Dean of Pixar University, Randy Nelson, states 'the skills we develop are skills we need everywhere in the organisation. Why teach drawing to accountants? Because drawing class doesn't just teach people to draw, it teaches them to be more observant. There's no company on earth that wouldn't benefit from having people become more observant.'

These conditions are similar to the beginning of the industrial revolution, only in this case it is the creative sector that can take forward the development of a better way of developing business, by being confident, leading, collaborating, making efforts to understand and changing the traditional business sector. The value of creative abilities should again take a central role within mainstream economics, and the value of creative activities equated and rewarded appropriately. For this to be successful the gap must be closed and the connections re-established.

This 'Lobotomy' of our minds is reversible. At a personal level we can deliberately get in touch with our creative side as they do at Pixar or take a good look at how we manage our lives and use our logical capacity to plan and improve. Changes can be made and new skills, even the administrative ones, can be learnt. We can become more tolerant and start to appreciate the vast diversity that has given us the wealth and success we have achieved. At a group level, more openness can be developed, prejudice reduced or even eliminated and stronger networks built. At an organisational level policies can be altered and new work practice adopted. We can do all these things. We know we can because we've already made changes like this for other types of prejudice such as race, gender and age, and because these changes are part of a new economic force that is sweeping the world, one that is every bit as powerful as the industrial age. The benefits are generational; we need to give our children the tools to build their world, instead of maintaining ours.

So what is getting in our way? Are we really that risk averse? Have we become entirely dependent on targets and performance indicators, and do we really trust in memory test results to tell us anything useful about a person's potential? Equally, have we become aloof and disconnected from the realities of commerce and progress? Has our world become so divided that we can no longer engage with people who have a different world view, maybe wear unique clothes, use different styles and have a language and style of their own? Are we using our cultural traits to advertise compliance and sameness? Is the lobotomy now ingrained within our day to day behaviours?

Part 3: Modern life

Part 3: Chapter 7: Language, lifestyles and dress codes

Just because you live in LA doesn't mean you have to dress that way

- Advertising billboard[59]

How you dress, style your hair, how you speak, how you communicate, how you work, how you relax and what type of lifestyle you live all contribute to the picture others see of you, and it affects how they react to you. Immediate judgements are made that we all seek to influence, and together these attributes project an image of who we want to be in the world. They act as communicators of status, wealth, education, interests and desires. Little wonder then that we can find plenty of evidence that our 'two-world' model of the creative and non-creative existence has hallmarks that distinguish one from the other. For example, in our experience, team meetings between creatives and business types were tense before anyone had spoken. Language and dress codes were used to define which group someone belonged to, and who had power. Seemingly superficial and idealistically of no importance, they can be fundamentally damaging to the aim of achieving productive collaboration. This is not to say that everyone needs to put away their personalities before any discussion takes place, but it does mean we need to appreciate what's happening and must not let it get in the way of our judgements.

Dress codes

Some of the ways in which we project which world we live in are very vivid and immediate. They act as a badge, letting others know who and what we are without having to say a word. If you're dressed as a member of the dominant ingroup then respect is in order, if not then maybe disdain or ridicule. While these stereotypical reactions have been portrayed many times in films and television, to ensure we get the character's role quickly, the impact on day-to-day life may not be so positive. A dress code can have intended and non-intended associations.

If you think about it there are obvious differences between the creative dress code and the traditional business dress code. Watch any TV episode of *Dragons' Den* or *The Apprentice* to see it played out. Or attend a music festival, such as Glastonbury in the UK or Burning Man in the Black Rock Desert, Nevada, USA, to see dress codes at the creative edges, but both have similar messages. Codes are used to inform others about our politics, beliefs, sexuality, awareness and preferences. They are part of human society - a tribal form of communication.

In any day we may swap to another set of clothes depending on events. In a curious reverse juxtaposition of roles, in the daytime many creatives dress down but in the evening they dress up to go to work or go out networking, whereas in the more conventional world of business, people dress up for work in the daytime (for networking) and in the evening dress down. Of course we are in part talking about those whose work involves night time entertainment, but there are still very different styles for the two groups. Standing on the edge of the 'divide', each group would not look the same at any given time of day. Small visual signals give us away; the way we accessorise our clothes or put them together, or how we wear our hair. Even with a school uniform these things are apparent. Do we polish our shoes or not? Not doing so can become a statement when worn in conjunction with a minor subversion of the uniform itself, for instance, and carry a very different meaning from unpolished shoes worn through lack of care. These nuances tend not to be picked up by an outgroup, hence the intended message and value is lost.

A dress code is of course the most visible factor to highlight the difference between our creative and our business communities. We make instant judgements about people based upon what they wear, so it is not surprising that this is a major component that fuels potential prejudice. Take, for example, this story from Mike relating his experience of dealing with dress styles during a recruitment campaign.

'Part of my job was to conduct interviews for new staff. Some candidates just "looked wrong". The culture of the place was closer to the city of London than the local community, so we had difficulty getting the right people. Tattoos, nose rings, bright clothes all sent the wrong message. This wasn't a "disapproval" - more a "how will they fit in with the existing team"? It wasn't easy to follow best practice recruitment processes that recommended tolerance and impartial assessment and at the same time try to find the best fit.'

We can all find examples of this sort of prejudice; however, dress codes are there for a reason. If we are going to work collaboratively we need to become much more tolerant of the way others present themselves but we also need to have more empathy with those we are intending to work with. Sure, if you want to join a rock band, probably turning up in a grey business suit isn't going to help no matter how good your playing is, and likewise if you want to pitch for a contract with a bank, turning up in torn jeans is likely to be a fast route to the down elevator. But because someone dresses differently from us does not necessarily mean that negative associations should be made, something that is all too common in both worlds.

Although many members of Richard Florida's creative class work in a hybrid environment of formality and creativity (particularly associated with IT companies) they are moving rapidly away from the suited look of the earlier decades. Very few women now wear tailored outfits, and for men chinos, trainers, and no ties are the more common look. Perhaps reflecting the intellectual component of their jobs, they begin to morph with university academic staff, as the links and interdependence become closer. These changes are shrinking the 'no-man's land' making it easier to exist in both worlds and removing the prejudicial associations.

At another level fashion can have a powerful impact on our lives. Fashion can provide us with the ability to be both compliant and unique - dressing as part of a group and sending the message that we wish to belong, or proclaiming our individuality. We can project a dual personality: fashion and anti-fashion[60]. Fashion moves in rebellious ways, and many creatives reflect its individualistic elements. Even when the grey suit becomes obsolete and unfashionable, it is replaced with another uniform that may have more colourful choices, but ultimately is a declaration of the same tribal belonging.

So important are these codes that, at the social level, our emotional and physical ambitions can be communicated. For example, desirability or sexual awareness can be communicated (or mis-communicated) through dress codes. Being aware of the role of dress codes, and getting the context right is an important part of reducing accidental friction.

Imagine you're a designer who's responded to a brief from a company who want a new logo. You arrive with your team, feeling proud of the fact that you've produced work of artistic excellence which will greatly enhance the company's standing. The style you have chosen for the logo is much better than what they've got at the moment. As you wait to be called in, you look around, aghast. There is sea of grey and blue sitting quietly tapping away at computer screens. They look like slaves, employees having to wear their uniform of dull business suits. You all feel proud to be able to show off your individual style and clothes, but you feel a little unnerved. Maybe you can help this company to loosen up a bit; these people really need your help. You walk in to the meeting room with your team. Sitting around the room are people all mostly wearing the same dark suits. They look up and seem hostile. You almost laugh, these people are deadbeats. You don't mind, they'll soon come round once they've seen your presentation.

Now contrast this with the views of the company director:

As the designers walk in, your employees, all dressed smartly in suits, try not to stare. They feel insulted that these people have not made any effort with their appearance. They are wearing jumpers with holes in, have wild hair and tattoos, look like they haven't washed and as far as you are concerned they probably all take drugs. They look very out of place in your office and highly unprofessional. They seem unable to sit on a chair properly. They show you their work and launch into a presentation about who they have worked for, rounding out with some high definition ideas that look way off. In fact, their ideas are revolutionary, and with a bit of negotiation would have made an impact, but they just haven't made any effort to meet your company halfway, are clearly not ready for the high prestige of working for you and are probably art students of some sort. So you offer them a small amount of money in view of the fact that doing work for you would look great on their CV. You would put a link on your website to them, they could think of it as a 'foot in the door'. You give them a few tips on design ideas and software programmes they could use, as they are obviously not a professional outfit and could use your help.

As you can see, the two camps can read the same situation very differently. The well-meaning creatives would feel horrified and sad to learn that their appearance was seen by the business types as 'insulting', and the business types would not be happy that their appearance was seen as threatening, dull and incomprehensible to the creatives.

Of course, in this situation both parties lose out. The stereotyping leads to misjudgements.

Language

Today, every sector has its own language - filled with acronyms, nuances, sayings, jargon and slang. The gap is further widened by the use of these different languages, each very sector-specific, and used to let people know what type of person we are and what kind of world we inhabit. Like dress codes, if you use the wrong language you are not going to succeed whilst the prejudice is still rampant and playing out. It is possible to commit a faux pas through use of language just as easily as adopting the wrong dress code.

The language of each sector can be difficult to understand if you're not used to it. Here's an example of 'business speak' from Mike:

'We aim to develop a commercial offer that will be attractive to the business community. The aim would be to re-energise a workforce or to enable positive change. Our key aims are to extend our reach into all areas of consumer life experiences, providing a professional vehicle to deliver policy ambitions and commercial sector improvements, whilst investing in professional development and creating sustainable positive change.'

Whereas Sue would be more likely to use language such as:

'People typically have a visceral response to my work (positive or negative) and "knowing" or "meaning" does not change that reaction.'

This technical language can be used like a weapon and can kill a piece of work stone dead. Here are two examples from Sue of how language problems nearly destroyed creative projects:

'I once managed a project where a theatre company were going to come in to work with the students in a college science department, teaching science via the methodology of theatre. The Head of Science had a meeting with the director of the company, in which they discussed what scientific terms and concepts needed to be taught to the students during the course of the project. However, after a few weeks the project still hadn't got off the ground and both sides were complaining about each other - in fact, the project nearly failed. It turned out to be because the theatre company hadn't explained the term "devised work" to the Head of Science. In theatrical terms, devising involves constructing a performance via a series of physical drama workshops, but the Head of Science was waiting for someone to send him the script of the play that his pupils would be performing.'

Had the theatre director suffered a degree of cultural lobotomy, expecting that everyone would understand the process of a devised way of working? Or was it the Head of Science assuming that everything would arrive on his lap, written down for him to check through? Either way, it illustrates a wide chasm between two mind-sets when people in such notable positions should be able to deal with each other's world.

Here's Sue's second example:

'I began to realise that there was some quite serious friction developing between me and my creative friends - once, at a meeting to discuss a community arts project, I told them that they might be eligible for funding if they measured the impact of their work according the school's educational objectives. But they just gave me a withering look. The words I had used sounded like "business speak" to them. I was using words like "advocacy" and "evaluating impact", whilst they were enthusiastically discussing the content of their proposed show. They didn't apply for the grant and the show consequently suffered from lack of resource.'

Finally, here is Mike realising that creative people need something different from what he is used to giving – an early lesson on how to begin closing the gap:

'I was beginning to realise that the creatives were not signed up, in fact they appeared to be actively hostile. The operatives would rather write a story than fill out an evaluation sheet. I couldn't remember the last time I had failed to get a message across at a business meeting. From boardrooms to team meetings I was good at it, usually because I'd done my homework, and networked with the key players beforehand. But something was nagging away. In business everyone uses Powerpoint, but in this creative setting everyone hated Powerpoint, full stop. Everyone. Also in business no-one cared about 'graphics' or clip art that much - they were a distraction from the information - text was the norm, but in this creative culture everyone cared about the graphics, text was almost obsolete. And the staff, what was going on there? Whatever it was, I needed to understand it.

'In the end I got some help from the creative community, who helped me redesign my presentations using unique graphic visualisations. I changed my language and dropped the business speak, introduced musical metaphors, organised games that related to our aims, and stopped turning up in a suit and tie - unless I was expected to talk to the board, then I needed a change of clothes'.

Lifestyles

The gap is further illustrated by the fact that creative and business people lead very different lives. The creative lifestyle often involves late nights, which may mean working until the early hours and having informal meetings in pubs, whereas the business lifestyle means early mornings, travelling to an office or workplace, and having formal meetings in that workplace.

A friend of Sue's, who is a stand-up comedian, tells this story:

'This journalist wanted an interview with me. I agreed and she said she'd give me a call at nine o'clock the next morning. I said "I don't do mornings". She said, "I'll ring you at 10 o'clock then." I said "I don't do mornings". "11 o'clock?" "Listen, love, I DON'T DO MORNINGS!"'

So, the journalist went away with the idea that the comedian is lazy and doesn't get out of bed until lunchtime. The comedian is miffed that the journalist expects him to fit into her 9-5 work pattern and doesn't understand that he doesn't get to bed until four in the morning.

They end up resenting each other. This is not to say that the journalist isn't creative, she is. But her lifestyle has always meant getting up early to meet her deadlines.

The two worlds are very different. In the office, it's a world of photocopying, filing, form filling, desks, chairs, timekeeping, management, duties, meetings, lunch, commuting, working with people, promotion, clothes, rules, bonuses, overtime and salaries. In the studio it can be a lonely existence, deadlines have to be met but time keeping usually means working late to get the job done, then taking a day or two off to recover.

Mike writes:

'I was a boss at the BBC. As glamorous as this may sound there was a wall right down the middle of the place. Creatives on one side, business on the other. The "suits" concerned with money drove the creatives round the bend. The resulting war landed the BBC in a world of strikes and mayhem, and only the consultants were happy. To keep all this machinery working, everyone obeyed protocol; tasks were completed in order, people you would never normally socialise with worked alongside you. It's an artificial environment – it has to be, in order for the corporation to function efficiently. The more I moved with the beat of the BBC the more this lifestyle began to dominate. Seduced by the power, status and seemingly unsolvable endless puzzles and games - my real life, the one containing my partner, children, friends, family and music, was getting infected'.

Juxtapose that against this, a story from Sue who went from leading a 'creative' lifestyle to a more 'business' type lifestyle, showing how difficult it can be to merge the two, and how the right- and left-brained ways of working are so very different

'As I had never bought any new furniture in my life and the concept seemed wasteful to me, I unsuccessfully trawled the second hand shops for a desk for my new office. The new temp. was both a lifesaver and a challenge. Having previously worked at an investment bank, she was corporate through and through. She persuaded me that buying brand new office furniture was not morally wrong, so we went to a specialist shop, where she strongly advised me against having pink chairs on the grounds that no-one in business would ever take me seriously. Eventually I went for a range of mixed colours, still defying her advice regarding a uniform navy blue look. She told me what was needed in an office – filing cabinets, lockable cupboards.

She was the first of several people who would be challenged by my lack of formal or "normal" management skills or behaviour. Bare feet in the office, eating bunches of parsley at my desk and a preference for flat hierarchies were all behaviours that challenged some of my team. The touring alternative theatre companies and bands I had been in did not operate management structures. With no management training, I was baffled by the need of some adults to be told what to do - especially in areas of which I had no knowledge – mainly admin and finance'.

It is clear that we need to begin to close the gap in terms of our dress codes, language and lifestyle. We have already mentioned that office dress codes are beginning to relax. However it can be very difficult to enter the world of the 'other side' and make that first approach. A photographer we talked to told us about a meeting that he had set up with someone who worked at Arts Council England. He wanted to invite the person he was meeting out to lunch, but because he had no experience of office protocol, he didn't know if people who worked in office were 'allowed out' at lunchtime. So he didn't ask, in case he showed his ignorance or caused embarrassment.

In general and certainly in the business world, our reward systems – what you get paid or what grades you get – are largely directed at the productive highly focused mind. Those who excel at this are given the highest rewards, but the wandering mind is where our creative thoughts take shape. A balanced healthy mind can do both, but this doesn't mean it *will* do both. We learn to do what we have to do. If we do not invest in our capacity to create, it will not develop the same expertise and capability as our focused concentrating mind. If we reinforce this with a lifestyle that is dedicated to concentrating on 'stay on message' performance, the room for creative thoughts and their beneficial effects on our mind will dissipate.

The balanced healthy mind enjoys day dreaming and wandering as much as task achievement and concentration. If a mind is almost permanently wandering, social tasks may well suffer, such as communicating with others. If a mind is permanently engaged in concentrated focused tasks, the chances are that nothing new will be able to take the place of the task once it's complete - except another task, probably allocated by something or someone else. Both extreme conditions are likely to cause personal problems. For example take an inability to perform day-to-day tasks leading to frustration and anger as deadlines are missed. Blame may be directed at the task or those who allocated it (bureaucracies or managers). This may have negative physical outcomes such as stress or an inability to relax, sleep and enjoy life as the task is always at the forefront of the mind. Similarly being totally task-driven may mean there is never any opportunity to imagine or create, leading to depression and anxiety and a lack of self-esteem.

As we mentioned previously, creatives tend to do their work by networking in the evenings rather than formal Monday morning meetings. Interestingly, coffee and other caffeine products suppress dopamine and make mind-wandering more difficult, and hence hamper creativity, whereas alcohol, in moderation, can enhance it.

These traits of lifestyle, dress code and language that betray our social preferences may seem to be just a veneer that masks the real issues. In our view they represent a reflection of how our world is moving in opposite directions. We celebrate diversity, welcome differences and embrace new ideas; we are designed to do that. When we close out opportunities, dismiss new ideas, exclude possibilities we are walking away from our future. We build unsupported myths around why we are what we are, such as 'only a few people are creative, only some people can make money, only some people can mange time successfully'. If history teaches us one thing, it is that the future is made today, and exploited tomorrow, by talented people.

Part 3: Chapter 8: Selling out v pure art

Ain't singin' for Pepsi
Ain't singin' for Coke
I don't sing for nobody
Makes me look like a joke

- Neil Young, *This Note's For You,* 1988

Selling out

The 20th century saw the development of a new lobotomising concept: somehow it has become possible for an artist to 'sell out'. This isn't the same as artistic integrity, although it is often linked to it. Selling out can involve being part of a TV commercial, having your work adapted for a mainstream film, having a hit record, and any number of similar financially successful events from sponsorship to collaborations. The relationship between those who accuse and those who are accused is confusing. In some cases those who may have been part of an artist's first success become agitated when the same artist achieves much wider success. In other cases critics may play a part, and in still others peer groups may accuse their comrades.

Sue writes;

'In 2011, I went to see the band *Public Image*. It was their comeback tour in London. My partner wouldn't come with me, because he'd seen Johnny Rotten in a butter advert on TV and was so outraged that he couldn't bring himself to come to the gig. His anti-establishment hero had apparently become part of the very system that he had always fought against. Johnny had "sold out". '

But had he? The butter company were using Johnny because people liked and respected him for everything he stood for. They were trying to sell us butter by exploiting Johnny's integrity for a commercial end. But is that really a problem? My partner bought the Public Image album despite the fact that the artist would get very little money from it; the record label, distributor and retailer get the lion's share. What is wrong with the artist actually making some money? Would people prefer that the band have no way to earn money, I wondered? Johnny was using the butter money to fund his tour. Why is that so bad? Does it make him some kind of a fake? He still needs to eat whilst getting his message across - regardless of which side his bread is buttered. In response to attitudes about selling out, fellow punk rocker Henry Rollins posted a video on YouTube highlighting exactly these points[61]. This was played to a group of creative practitioners, after seeing the famed butter ad. 'Tutting' through the butter ad then listening to Rollins changed a lot of minds, but not all, who still felt that the Rotten's credibility had been compromised by associating with a commercial company.

How did being creative and the business of making money become separated? Why do we judge people or ourselves in this way?

Earning a living from creativity almost certainly means electing to be an entrepreneur. After all, the products of the individual's creativity are now for sale; it is an inescapable fact. Being successful means having great products as well as being good at selling them, in short being creative and being an entrepreneur. However, if the marketplace is altered so that there is little need to sell, as is the case with public funding and grants, then the creative community is at liberty to develop layers of elitism, attaching value to the 'purity' of what they do rather than its market value. Is that ok? There are no successful entrepreneurs in other market sectors that don't 'sell' their products.

The Muse

In ancient Greece creativity in arts and literature was understood to be the result of being inspired by a *muse*[62]. This external God-like force was the root of all new thoughts and gave the creator the freedom to blame the muse if things did not go well, but also prevented the creator from taking all the credit! Even modern-day musicians pay homage to the concept. Tom Waits relates how he was driving home when an idea for a song started to come to him: 'Hey can't you see I'm driving! Go see Leonard Cohen!' was his response. This concept has links to Eastern philosophy where creativity of any sort is simply a truth being revealed. The skill of the creator is to be able to peel away the layers that obscure the truth. In the West we have developed a different view, that creativity belongs to or is a central ability of the individual. This allows an individual or group to exploit the products of creativity as their 'property'. Intellectual property rights are enshrined in law, and are a fundamental part of many businesses, having expression as unique products, protected by trademarks and patents.

'Johnny Rotten' could be seen as just a brand name for John Lydon. If the muse were at the root of all creative activity then 'Johnny Rotten' could simply become one product, while John Lydon remains intact. Returning to the butter ad, it could be said that Lydon can do a butter ad, whereas Rotten cannot. This type of thinking could be a useful tool for artists, allowing them to branch out and be more entrepreneurial. The muse model also has other benefits. It is good for the mental health of artists, as the pressure is off - if you are not visited by the muse, you cannot be creative - and you have someone else to blame things on if your work is not up to scratch[63].

And of course while selling out might seem a luxury attitude, more to do with emotions than commerce, the activities of the underlying business continue unfettered. John Lydon's band the Sex Pistols didn't make any money. Did anyone complain? All the anarchistic punks who bought album after album and paid for tickets to shows, did they storm the offices of EMI or Virgin records demanding that their heroes be recompensed for their music? The average record deal in 1980 gave the artists just 7% of sales. This 7% was often paid *net* of expenses. Expenses included all promotion costs, advertising, parties, booze, and transport – all business expenses incurred by the record label. The songwriters did better as their royalties were paid through a different channel, unless they signed a publishing deal with the same label. Nowadays it's even worse – artists are asked to sign a 360 degree deal, which allows the managers to take a cut from all the songwriting and performance sources as well, so the artists are worse off than they were back then.

The overall picture is not good. Yes, you can create something unique and beautiful, but when it is time to exploit it commercially the 'no selling out' rule is that you can't do this yourself, it has to be done by a separate business so you can remain pure and broke in your artistic garret.

So pervasive is the attitude and values that have developed around the term 'selling out' that Wikipedia has an entry for it:

> *'Selling out' is the compromising of (or the perception of compromising) integrity, morality, or principles in exchange for money or 'success' (however defined). It is commonly associated with attempts to tailor material to a mainstream audience. Any artist who expands their creative path to encompass a wider audience, as opposed to continuing in the genre and venues of their initial success, may be disdainfully labelled by disapproving fans as a sellout. Sometimes a sellout is seen as a person that is disloyal to one's group that he or she belongs (usually ethnic group) in order to gain money or become 'successful'. Selling out is often seen as gaining success at the cost of credibility[64].*

The term as applied to creative artists is new. It is a product of our modern view of what is valuable and what is not, how commercialism works, and our views of 'purity'. The reaction of rock band Green Day sums up an artist's pragmatic response:

> 'The fact was we got to a point that we were so big that tons of people were showing up at punk-rock clubs, and some clubs were even getting shut down because too many were showing up. We had to make a decision: either break up or remove ourselves from that element. And I'll be damned if I was going to flip fucking burgers. I do what I do best. Selling out is compromising your musical intention and I don't even know how to do that.'

Basically everyone else is allowed to make money doing what they do best, so why can't I?

The journeymen and women and masters and mentors of the craft guilds of the 15th and 16th centuries would not recognise the term or its underlying principle. They worked to order as well as to fulfil their own creative direction. Contracts were never turned down on the grounds that it would compromise artistic integrity as this attitude would have lead to financial ruin. So where did 'selling out' come from? Why do we want to cut down those artists who have made their success through commercial means?

Tall poppies

A component of 'selling out' is insidiously linked to a desire to cut people down to size. The term is often expressed as cutting down the 'tall poppies'; the term 'tall poppy' refers to those in a community who have excelled. Aristotle uses the concept of removing 'tall poppies' to illustrate the behaviour of dictatorial Roman emperors who maintained their power by killing eminent citizens who had too much influence. The term appears in modern parlance in politics and has become embedded in a debate about equality and policy. In 1931, Jack Lang, the Australian prime minister, made use of the phrase to explain his egalitarian politics and since then Australians have been accused of killing off their finest! However, Australians argue, they cut down tall poppies only if they act in an arrogant or aloof manner. 'A person can have great talent or prowess and if they combine that with humility or self-deprecating humour they will not be cut down'. Evidence of this can be seen in the success of Kylie Minogue, Hugh Jackman, Ian Thorpe, Dick Smith and Steve Irwin. Australians do not begrudge success to those who do not act above themselves. It is the attitude not the success that determines the cultural reaction.

Pure art

The purity of art relates strongly to the concept of selling out. You can't sell out unless there is some underlying state that is more acceptable or moral than the one you're proposing to enter. The purity of art stems from a 19th century term 'Art for Art's sake'; a term credited to the French writer and poet Théophile Gautier (1811–1872). It represented the beginning of a movement to distance art from everyday human activity including commerce, and was probably the first serious step towards lobotomising our minds. Art was seen as a means to serve some high moral purpose. It implied that art was valuable simply as art, that artistic pursuits were their own justification, that art did not need moral justification and was allowed to be morally subversive. A surprisingly contemporary criticism of the phrase and its attendant moral code was made by Nigerian novelist Chinua Achebe in his collection of essays entitled *Morning Yet on Creation Day* (1975) where he asserts that 'art for art's sake' is 'just another piece of deodorised dog shit'. Yet the seeds of 'selling out' are sown. The new commercialisation and the need for art to find another meaning drive the appearance of a code that creates a new elitist place for art.

Survival

On the face of it these behaviours and attitudes look like commercial suicide. What is keeping these people alive, while the rest of us are working our socks off? The 19th and 20th centuries have seen the creation of welfare states, particularly in the new economies of the West. It could be argued that this provides the safety net that gives artists the ability to avoid commercialism and embrace a purist integrity. Now it is possible to both survive and claim a purity for your art that doesn't require the tainted world of buying and selling to provide an income.

We were told this story by a British university lecturer:

> 'I was asked by the university to run a number of workshops for the fine arts department to sensitise the students to the marketplace for their work. Part of the workshop took the form of each student running a stall where the students' work would be displayed and could be sold to the public. But I was told by the arts faculty, "Oh no, that's not the sort of thing we want our students to do, as it could interfere with the quality of the work"'.

How these students were supposed to make a living after their course was apparently of no concern to the tutors who considered the world of commerce to be beneath them, or certainly not within their remit.

This luxurious elitism is unsustainable; the concept of 'selling out' is no longer a relevant or pragmatic survival strategy. Today artists are collaborating commercially on many new fronts. A recent comment made by a band manager at the South by South West music conference in Austin, Texas USA indicates a change. 'Last year only two of my roster of bands would consider a sponsorship deal, this year they all would'. Modern savvy consumers employ social media to communicate and brands know that music is the main factor in driving activity among social media sites. Hooking your wagon to a cool band is now a good idea. Getting on board earlier and helping to develop their career may be an even smarter strategy, as when their fans come you want to be there, you don't want to be standing in a doorway wondering where everyone has gone. The game is get in front of the public; who brings them doesn't really matter.

We are beginning to see justifications for collaborations and sponsorship that make far more sense than the 'selling out' accusations. Here is an example from blogger Seth Stevens about ex-Beatle, Sir Paul McCartney, who appeared in an advert for Fidelity Insurance:

'*What he's doing in that Fidelity ad?*

'*I think Paul's driving desire is for relevance. This is a way for Paul to say "Remember that bloke in the home-movie clips? The guy you loved so much? I'm still here. I've got a fresh new album. I hope you'll actually listen to it". (McCartney plays all the instruments on several tracks of this album release,* 'Chaos and Creation in the Backyard', *suggesting the work might be especially close to his heart.) It's odd that one of the most famous figures of the 20th century is doing mutual-fund ads just to stay in the public eye. But that's showbiz. And can we really consider it selling out when what you crave above all else is to put your new art in front of your audience'?*

In a BBC TV interview in 2010 Paul also stated that he can't get any radio play. This meant that the main channel of music promotion is closed to him, maybe because of his age or the attitude of radio producers. Fronting an international ad campaign seems like a smart move. Paul is not only an accomplished musician, he is a smart entrepreneur.

Invariably his appearance at the 2012 London Olympics prompted the usual gaggle of snobbish responses including a spoof advert. As an aside, did you know that most of the musicians asked to play at the London Olympics 2012 had to play for free? However, the security firm was paid £286m, and as we know, screwed up big time.

Integrity

On balance the next story has a lot to do with artistic integrity and not so much to do with selling out, although both elements are in play. Every artist is entitled to decide how their products get used (or misused). It is only when they react against commercial exploitation just because it is commercial that they fall into the selling out trap. It illustrates how Western intellectual property gets used (or abused) and on the face of it seems to suggest commercial suicide.

Alan Moore is a well-known creator of comic books and graphic novels. With such a wealth of highly developed comic book concepts to his credit, it's surprising that none was transferred to the silver screen until 2001, and that the first was to be the lesser-known *From Hell*. *The League of Extraordinary Gentlemen* came next in 2003, *V for Vendetta* in 2006, and *Watchmen* in 2009.

Perhaps even more surprising is Moore's increasingly vitriolic reactions to these Hollywood adaptations, refusing to accept money for the film rights and demanding that his name be removed from the movie credits - particularly because Moore hasn't even viewed any of the various Hollywood film adaptations of his work. Quote 'I've never wanted to, and there's absolutely no chance of me doing so in the future.'

From early in his career, Moore understood that his work could not be successfully translated into film. Moore met with director Terry Gilliam, who had been enlisted to adapt Watchmen, and he asked Moore how he would do it. 'Well, frankly, Terry, if anybody had bothered to consult me before this point, I would have said, "I wouldn't'".

From Hell starred Johnny Depp, and is a pale shadow of Moore's masterpiece. Stripped down from a six-hundred-page graphic novel to fit the length of a two-hour movie, it inexplicably reduces the multilayered treatise on a serial killer and a parable about the misuse of power into a straightforward whodunit.

From Hell was a moderate success, and although Moore had become 'a little aggravated' about becoming associated with 'a film that was about something completely different' from his original work, he signed an option agreement for *The League of Extraordinary Gentlemen* to be made into a film. However, for legal reasons he was then ordered to write a new version of the comic, *The League of Extraordinary Gentlemen*, to fit in with what the film would now be. The new one was to feature a group of figures from Victorian literature including Dorian Gray and Tom Sawyer, neither of whom appeared in the original comic version of League; nor did any of the original comic's characters feature in the screenplay; there was an accusation that the film company had plagiarised ideas from a screenplay called *A Cast of Characters*.

Moore was horrified at the potential damage to his reputation: 'I don't have the highest opinion of Hollywood screenwriters and for someone to suggest that I get my ideas from American movies is an intolerable affront'.

Twentieth Century Fox eventually settled with the plaintiffs out of court, which Moore viewed as virtually an admission of guilt. Moore immediately announced that he no longer wanted any of his works to be adapted to film: 'I felt, if I'm going to react, I might as well overreact'.

Unfortunately, he could not prevent the rights to his works controlled by DC Comics being sold to Hollywood producers due to the terms of his original contracts with the publisher signed in the early 1980s. And despite *The League*'s disastrous box-office failure, *V for Vendetta,* and *Watchmen* were each subsequently to become big-budget movies.

Unable to stop the films being made, Moore announced, 'I will not be accepting any money from those films, and I will be asking for my name to be removed from them'. He went on to say, 'All of the money due to me will go to the artists involved. I'm divorcing myself from the film process, the film industry, and any adaptations'.

Being interviewed on a BBC radio show, Moore told the audience that it was worth giving up the film money just for the look on Hollywood producers' faces as they wondered, 'If he doesn't want the money, what does he want?'

Moore is scathing about the sums involved in Hollywood movies; *Watchmen* reputedly cost over $200 million to make, and Moore suspects it was considerably more than that. 'You're talking hundreds of millions of dollars of which it recouped next to nothing. And this is in a world that is falling to bits'. Moore believes that such huge sums would have been better spent on trying to cure the world's ills, like civil unrest in Haiti or shoring up the levees in New Orleans rather than on 'dopey films that are just meant to fill another couple of hours of some over-privileged Western teenager's largely empty existence... can we afford to do films anymore? I know we still will, whether we can afford to or not'.

Critics

Critics infest the world of creativity. It is in their interest to build castles of imagined value and worth around those they find temporarily agreeable and meet the current fashion or trend. These trends are often invented to massage an ego, or establish a daring stance. The most successful artists are often the target of such vitriol. The outcome for the mainstream is to make the arts seem unworldly, aloof, elitist and irrelevant. No wonder the arts community spend much of their political time defending public funding and completing grant applications.

Jack Vettriano is self-taught artist, born in Scotland. As Lawrence Pollard, the BBC World Service arts critic puts it: 'It would be hard to find an artist more scorned, mocked and abused by established critics. But it would also be as hard to think of another living painter whose images have spread so far round the world. In commercial terms he can be ranked as the world's most successful living painter'.

'I've set the scene, you build the story', Vettriano told BBC World Service on the *Today* programme. 'What I'm trying to do is set up these little dramas. I'm like a film director who's only going to give you one shot, that's it, and it's up to you to finish the film on my behalf'. Most of the criticisms stem from his 'untrained' status. The art establishment (every bit as nefarious as the politburo) felt threatened by his success, using their most juvenile poison to undo his achievements. Like a mob of rabid bullies aiming ink pellets at the boy who is top of the class. 'Painting by numbers' was one of their most barbed attempts along with the more asinine 'derivative', 'pornographic' and 'simple-minded'.

The bigger man always turns away from this name-calling, sticks and stones. However they scored with one criticism. Vettriano says 'Someone wrote I was free to do what I liked so long as I understood "they wouldn't take me seriously". Who do they think they are?'

Veteran London critic Richard Cork wrote: 'I think the public turn to him with relief, thinking here's something they can understand, that they can take in almost at a glance, That's actually one of the problems I have with Vettriano - speaking as an art critic - I feel that once I have glanced at it I've got it really, there's not much more to appreciate'. And this from Jonathan Jones of The *Guardian*, 'I think his pictures are emotionally trite and technically drab, so they damage the cause of the painter'[65].

It's one easy step from this elitist position to an accusation of selling out. All an artist has to do is be popular and successful, and the pack will stand, noses raised as if there is a noxious odour that only they have noticed. For many of us though it is clear where the smell is coming from.

The value created by critics and reviewers is aimed at filtering the best, so we as consumers are presented with new, innovative, fresh and challenging content. However, losing the connection between our two personalities and becoming unbalanced leads to a corruption of the role. A key question must be, if another individual is dictating your tastes in art, then something is amiss – it's up to you to decide what's right or wrong for you, not a peer group who have little interest in artists' successes, but a lot in their own.

Encore

The new zeitgeist doesn't include the concept of 'selling out'. Contemporary business methods are being invented by the new information industries and the related creative industries and the people within them. These methods, values and behaviours are being taken up by traditional industries that want to survive the new revolution. Dreamworks is a creative company, so are 3M, Toyota, and CD Baby. The new ways of doing business are being forged by trail-blazers in the new creative science and media industries. In these new businesses 'rules' include sponsorship, product endorsements, being successful but not excessive, being smart but not arrogant. Banks should take note here! The programmer using Javascript to develop an iPhone app is just as cool as the guitarist, keyboard player and drummer in the latest cool band. Welcome to the new wave of creativity. Still believe in selling out, aloof artistic purity and elitist arrogance? Still think the old business methods are the way forward? There's a box for you. It's called obsolete.

Part 3: Chapter 9: The money myth

Now look at them yo-yos, that's the way you do it

You play the guitar on the MTV.

That ain't working, that's the way you do it

Money for nothing and your chicks for free

Dire Straits: *Money For Nothing*:
1985 single release from 'Brothers In Arms' Album[66].

Money management – myths and truths

This is the most successful Dire Straits single based on chart position. It reached number 1 in the US and Canadian charts and number 4 in the UK. For a short time the band had become the biggest act in the world. Mark Knopfler, the band's leader and virtuoso guitarist, finally split the band in 1995, having kicked the whole thing off in 1977 from Deptford, an inauspicious but creative South London suburb. The band wrote and rehearsed at Woodwharf studios, with a glorious view of the river Thames, and played pool at the pub next door. Their first gig was at the Albany Empire, now a rebuilt theatre and arts venue. In 2009 a special blue plaque was erected at Farrer House, Church Street in Deptford where the original group, Mark Knopfler, David Knopfler, John Illsley and Pick Withers once shared a council flat.

The lyrics to *Money For Nothing* comment on the stereotypical view of rock stars – a view that has been applied to many of the creative arts - it all looks easy, overpaid and certainly not like real work. In fact the work rate required to be the world's most successful band was one of the reasons they gave it all up. Seems crazy doesn't it, all that money.

Low pay no pay

The truth about creative work is it isn't well paid, up to now at least. It is generally very arduous, involving long hours of painstaking practice, dedication, trial and error. A serious creator needs to master their chosen craft. Many entry level jobs in the traditional creative sector pay expenses only (and in some cases not even that). In contrast to traditional career jobs, unpaid internships are common, which helps to explain why many creative industries are predominantly staffed by the white middle classes. It is only those groups whose parent(s) have sufficient funds to keep their children in jobs where they receive little or no pay. There is always the hope that one day they will be offered something tangible before they give up.

Internship is rife in the creative world. It's a practice inherited from the legal profession, where it was viewed as a form of apprenticeship with the promise of a paid job at the end. While the legal profession may still offer this route to a career, the creative sector invariably does not. Internships are now widely used as a way of getting free labour, especially in the arts and creative industries. This prompted the tax authorities in the UK to investigate breaches of the UK minimum wage laws, an intervention that has led some improvements. The 'Arts Jobs' website, run by the UK Arts Council, used to list two sections - one for paid and another for unpaid work, both equally populated with opportunities. Not so now, only paid opportunities appear, and a stiff guideline is posted warning employers about breaking UK minimum wage rules.

Ross Perlin, a veteran of the unpaid internship and a researcher for the Himalayan Languages Project in China, decided three years ago to investigate some of the issues that arise when these conflicting interests collide. What he found can be inferred through the title of his book– Intern Nation: *How to Earn Nothing - and Learn Little in the Brave New Economy*[67]. In an interview with *Inside Higher Ed* he states, "I find the internships lacking on a number of levels, they have become this key gateway into the white collar work force ... but at the same time, access has become drastically unequal." Over the last few decades, thanks to globalisation and an economy in flux and over-credentialing, internships have become increasingly important for college graduates. But shoddy practices, little regulation and negligible or nonexistent wages have made it difficult for low-income students to compete with their more fortunate peers, he found. As Perlin intimates, internships are spreading to all industries. The role of schools and education in promoting these 'opportunities' also comes under fire:

"I do think that schools have to look at what they're doing in terms of promoting unpaid, unstructured opportunities at for-profit companies that seem to be illegal under US labor law," Perlin said. "It's something that we really need to pay attention to, and is a contributor at the deepest level to widening inequality."

In the UK a shake-up is underway, and those that abuse internships are being targeted. As reported in the *Guardian* newspaper (Thursday 17 November 2011) internal documents from Her Majesty's Revenue and Customs (HMRC) show that it believes interns *across the employment spectrum* to be at 'high risk' of abuse under national minimum wage laws. As a result HMRC has convened a 12-person taskforce to make unannounced inspections of businesses where interns are being used as workers rather than just shadowing staff. The special dynamic response unit will have powers to question managers and sift through accounts until it is satisfied that no abuse is taking place. It is the first time intern abuse has been targeted by the HMRC, which is responsible for the enforcement of the minimum wage. It follows heavy criticism from the UK Low Pay Commission over the lack of enforcement action. Companies, such as clothes store Urban Outfitters, have in the past advertised for nine-month unpaid internships. Topshop, owned by billionaire Sir Philip Green, also offers month-long unpaid internships although it says the role only involves shadowing employees, not actual work. Fashion house Vivienne Westwood has previously advertised for a three-month unpaid internship which required a high level of prior IT skills from would-be applicants. The HMRC internal briefing document also highlights the growing nature of the intern problem. It says that over the past few years there has been a significant rise in the number of UK employers offering internships. It adds that the HMRC should target the fashion industry for the next six months because it is 'well known for the use of interns'. The *Guardian* recently revealed government lawyers had advised Department of Business ministers that 'most interns are likely to be workers and therefore entitled to the [national minimum wage] and other worker rights'. An HMRC source told the *Guardian* it would be targeting a range of firms, from the multinationals to the smallest design company. 'If you are in that industry and you have interns, there's no reason to think that we won't be knocking on your door', they said.

So far has the internship disease spread that in 2010 in the UK over 92% of jobs in the arts sector were offered as unpaid internships, and many required graduate qualifications. In the public sector too, more and more jobs are being created where expenses are the only reward, sometimes in a cynical attempt to reduce unemployment figures for the young. Having lobotomised our creative mind and devalued our creative activities to the point where we no longer pay anyone for carrying out creative work, the financial trick is being taken up by other sectors. The logical conclusion must be that workers will eventually be paid nothing, but will be supported by their parents or the government, while company directors receive larger and larger bonuses for delivering a zero-cost operation. You could be forgiven for considering this strategy a form of madness.

Adding up

The creative sector and those that work in it have a reputation for not understanding or managing their money well. However it probably applies to most people irrespective of their work, given the numbers of people who have made little or no pension provision, invested in fraudulent companies or simply failed to save anything for that rainy day. But there are likely to be issues if a mind-set has been established that rejects logical brain activities as being destructive in terms of creativity; if in short the lobotomy has devalued the capabilities that we all have to work out the money stuff.

Stereotypically creative types have a reputation for flaky money management. Also there are issues about normal business practice such as general admin, getting back to people, answering their emails and so on. This leads to one wondering how they can make a living. The answer is that in many cases they don't – they just scrape by, and often their income comes from sources other than their creative work – so one often finds actors working at dull menial jobs in restaurants and bars in order to pay the bills, never committing themselves to anything more demanding or with more responsibility in case their big break arrives.

Even today in art schools and colleges little is taught about how to apply the arts out there in the commercial world. This bit of making a living is considered dirty work. Because of this attitude the 'how to make a living' bit is often missing from arts courses. Graduates risk becoming reliant on state support with occasional periods of self employment and so continue to have little to do with the world of making money and building a future. This does not mean it is any harder to make a living in the arts than it is anywhere else, business is after all business. Simply put, the people working in this sector may not have the skills to be successful. Once this culture is established, the arts begin to appear as an economic backwater, they are challenged to justify any further investment, and they are vulnerable to inappropriate performance targets. Our research shows that while creative people are happy to pay for training around their art form, they will not pay for training in business skills or money management as they consider it much less valuable. They will only concentrate on the subjects that they like, and ignore the others, exhibiting the kind of 'silo thinking' that tends to emerge in secondary schools where learning is delivered in subject-based lessons rather than as an integrated whole. Turning away from their logical selves, the part we all need to manage our daily lives, leads to economic failure.

Of course this creates problems - if someone else has to manage the money it is easy to attract the less scrupulous. This manifests itself in the form of treatment handed out to artists by managers, agents and other business intermediaries. For example many musicians have experienced fraudulent or unfair treatment at the hands of their management or record labels.

It wasn't good in the early days when the music business expanded on the back of unrivalled success in the 60s and 70s, after all even the Beatles had to take their record company to court.

Sue writes from her own experience in the 1980s as a young member of a successful theatre music troupe:

'There were the recording costs for that elusive hit single to pay for, and of course the manager's fees. We didn't know how much we were making or where the money was going – we were grateful for the £40 a week 'wage' our management paid us. Sometimes they took us out to dinner and we had bottles of wine that cost more than we were paid in a month. It never occurred to me that it was our earnings that were paying for all this. The management had the auditors in once and our wages were frozen. Eventually we went in and demanded some money as we couldn't pay the rent. I remember the look on our manager's face when it gradually dawned on him that we were actually living on that £40 a week and had no savings to fall back on. He had been a millionaire by the time he was 21, so what did he know? '

'It wasn't that we were daft. It was just that it wasn't in the culture of being a creative person to be on top of your finances. To be good at that would somehow be selling out, and becoming part of the system that you were supposed to be against. Our lifestyle just didn't fit into the system - and this provided further ammunition for our resentment and alienation. 'Basically we had a naivety about business which is common to most creative people - but why did we?'

More soup please

The film industry operates a multi billion pound business. Most feature-length films make money (eventually). At the top end the industry pays rates agreed with unions and the staff. This ensures that the people who make the film are rewarded. However at the entry level much work is done free of pay. The films are made with little funding and the workers are often working for no pay, trying to get experience to add to their show reel. However in the UK this is largely the norm creating an endless plea for financial help. This situation has prompted Lord Putnam, chair of the British Film Council, to observe that the UK film industry has a 'soup kitchen' mentality[68] – looking for hand-outs when it should be writing business cases and interesting serious investors. Unfortunately most of the film making community in the UK avoids this vital step. Why?

Television, radio and print media are heavily reliant on similar models. Theatre has a similar culture.

Compare this picture with the new creative engineering and science industries – information technology, games, video and web design. Here the rewards are high. Here are the new creatives, defining how we should be working. Highly valued by their customers these skills are in demand.

Greed

Since the 1990s a new reward culture has exploded in the boardrooms across the world: the culture of bonus payments. Following the shift in business objectives from achieving profitability and growth to building shareholder value, executives now reward themselves for achieving share price gains, sometimes even when nothing has been achieved. This translates into salaries of millions of dollars for board members. Executive pay is now over 100 times that of the average employee. This has happened quickly, and has created even greater inequality and consequent anger. Recently fast food company Macdonald's has suffered a strike by its workforce who are among some of the lowest paid in the US. It is estimated that the ratio of salary to executive pay at MacDonald's is over 1000:1[69].

For many of us money is a mystery, or at least the way we use it or allow it to be used seems mysterious. Money appears to be at the root of some big problems.

What is money?

Money in its raw state is nothing more than printed paper bank notes, but add the social maelstrom where money is used to transact deals and build dreams, and the picture changes. Money is a representation of wealth and power. It can affect our well-being and impact our happiness and health. There is an emotional connection between money and our lives. Think how secretive we are about our earnings, our pension plans and our savings and investments. Think how we view people who seem to have lots of money and those who don't. Think how we feel when we are short of money and when we are not. Think how greed and philanthropy arise.

Money is a major cause of worry and distress, for example it may lie at the heart of a couple's arguments, or be touted as the reason for inaction or anger. We invent stories around it, we speculate 'if only', we dream. It plays a part in our success but we also try to make it do things it cannot do: succinctly put as *'money can't buy me love'*. Why then are so many well educated and competent people financially illiterate[70]? Understanding money is a necessary skill. Without it we are doomed to make mistakes and may find it much harder to get what we want, risking a life of poverty. Take for example the person who is trying to make ends meet, perhaps trying to raise a family on a very low income. Careful money management is essential. But examples of rash spending and poor budgeting are common. Take the entrepreneur trying to establish a business, or those who aim to retire before they are 70. All these people need to manage money, and understand how it works. Too many people know far too little about money. The reasons for this are historical. To date, education has not included money management. This is changing; in the UK the topic has been introduced into the national curriculum. Money if managed well can help us to achieve what we want. It is not the reason that there is good and evil in the world, we need to disentangle the emotional from the practical.

Money is our life story, we constantly use it to satisfy our needs and plan for our future. There is an endless dialogue going on. For example, if we decide not to save for our retirement we have decided to be poor when we are old.

But it is not just we as consumers who need to raise our game.

Money money money

Since 2008 the world has suffered a financial catastrophe. In capitalist democracies, money is supposed to be used to fund the next phase of economic development – airports, bridges, new industries etc. This is the same as using our savings to fund a new house. Instead most of the world's capital (savings) was used to fund fraudulent projects such as the sub-prime mortgage industry in the

US and speculate on the future price of commodities. This money was lost. The original cash plus the interest which will never be paid has evaporated. This is a bit like buying a holiday and finding out the holiday firm was bogus, so no holiday. As it was the banks that did this, they are now short of money. As the banks are supposed to fund economic growth, economic growth is reduced and we all enter an economic recession. Strangely in the financial capital London, the centre of the 'fraud', no one has been prosecuted. In the USA many have been indicted and imprisoned, in Iceland governments have been changed.

Unfortunately it's not over yet. The consequences will be played out for many years, and future generations will suffer as a result.

It is a myth that we need to leave the management of our money to financial experts. We don't. For most of us a few standard bits of knowledge will work. Claiming that it's all too difficult or that we're not good at figures is an excuse, not a reason. The level of maths needed is elementary; there are many sources of information on the subject[71] suited to all levels of knowledge and abilities.

Getting money for your business

In October 2013 a music business conference took place at Somerset House in London[72], aimed at explaining finance to music businesses and launching a new guide. It was prompted by the low level of financial understanding within the music business. There are a number of ways a new business can gain funding and support; most of these avenues are used regularly by traditional business. The organisers' main aim was to raise the level of competence and awareness among young music business entrepreneurs.

Traditionally, small enterprises in the creative sector have relied on grants and even social security support for some of their incubation period, but many fail. Elsewhere a much wider set of funding options are used, which expect competent money management to assist success. This boils down to knowing how much is needed and why, spending it carefully and monitoring progress.

So what's on offer these days? Most of these types of funding are self explanatory:

Crowdfunding: Get a ton of people to contribute small amounts. Useful for one-off projects such as film or music, art exhibitions etc. Web sites such as Kickstarter and Indiegogo provide the technical platform to gather contributions and distribute the funds. This is becoming a very successful form of funding for creative projects, and start-up businesses.

Friends and family: Often a good way to raise some largely riskless capital.

Debt funding: Start a limited company and sell the shares to investors who will then own part of your company: This is the 'Dragon's Den' model based on selling equity in a company.

Grants: Available through philanthropic organisations such as the Macarthur foundation[73].

Government support: Depending where you live there may be free business support and links to low cost loans on offer.

Of course practical advice is always on offer. However if you start from a 'money is evil' standpoint (essentially an emotional assessment) then success is unlikely.

The impact of the cultural lobotomy on the management of money is twofold. Firstly we give up trying to manage it because it is beyond our capabilities, which is nonsense. Secondly we ascribe to it negative values, thereby claiming it and the world of money are against us, or against the values we stand for. However, the values we have can be amplified by money. If we have high social values money can be used to expand this, through philanthropy for example. If we have low morals money can amplify this too. In short money is agnostic; it is us who have values and beliefs not bits of paper with watermarks.

Crossing the river

For any funding options to work, a plan is needed. Planning involves three things: time, money and specification. These three elements compete, that is there will be limits on time and money that will constrain the specification. Specification is all about what you want to achieve. The plan will show when it can be achieved and at what cost.

And of course our time is precious. There are things we would rather do, and tasks we do not enjoy. Both money and time must be managed well – bad time management can drive us nuts.

Part 3: Chapter 10: The time myth

'Five minutes thought is worth a week's work'

- Popular sayings

'For disappearing acts, it's hard to beat what happens to the eight hours supposedly left after eight of sleep and eight of work.'

- Doug Larson

Time management – myths and truths

There are a number of sayings about time and work. Some are 'laws'. For example 'work will expand to fill the time available' is known as Parkinson's Law[74] – or said another way 'the amount of time which you have to perform a task is the amount of time it will take to complete the task'.

This pessimistic view could be tempered by including 'if you let it' at the end of the sentence, thereby adding a pinch of optimism.

Time is a fact of life. Well, physicists may argue that it isn't quite so clear cut, but for most of us we know what it is. It may not be easy to explain it, but we understand how it affects us. We sense that we move through time, our lives are calibrated by it, we can measure it and we can foresee it as a bounded period in which we will live the rest of our lives. We can conceptualise it as infinite, and we can fantasize about journeys through time, slowing it down and speeding it up. We can talk about the past and place our age and memories in it. We can be emotional about it. For example, we can become annoyed when someone is late, we can become perplexed when things we want to achieve take too long, we can become sad or joyful when remembering past events. We may find that we don't have enough time for everything we want to do, or that we have to give too much time to something we don't enjoy. There is a feeling that time belongs to us, and that we share this time with others. Time may also have a value or a price; being paid a fee of £40 per hour for example, or being charged for overdue parking.

Time is something we definitely want to manage. If we can get to grips with it then perhaps we can have a more enjoyable lifetime. Strangely we are sometimes aware that we have less time than we used to, we talk about modern life speeding up or not having time to do everything we need to. Somehow our lives have become busier. Oddly, the past, even the recent past in the 20th century, seems like a time when there was 'more time'. Looking back we can study a period when many new ideas and inventions flowed and new freedoms were won, yet somehow life was less busy.

Time tools

Time sometimes feels like it is out of control or at least out of our control. It can depress us and we may suffer from time-related anguish, be accused of procrastination or be angry with ourselves for missing a deadline. It can feel like time itself is a monster that drives us relentlessly, as we are encouraged to manage our time well. The digital age provides us with tools that may help, there is a ton of software available to help with time management. A lot of it will run on a smartphone: calendars, e-mails, spreadsheets and more exotic tools such as text prediction and voice activation are all included as standard on many makes and models. Together they provide a set of useful processes that help to keep us informed about the status of our tasks, including how much time we have left to complete them. These tools are also easy to use, and are so readily available, surely there is no excuse for not getting stuff done any more? So unless we are buried inside a complex corporate project surrounded by sliding deadlines and raging bosses, time management tools may help to control the beast.

Of course to really manage time we need more than a set of tools, we also need a set of skills. 'Time management' and its twin sister 'project management' and their uncle 'prioritisation' and second cousin 'pareto' (the 80/20 rule) and a whole collection of increasingly complex techniques are designed to get stuff done in order dictated by importance. These tools help in many situations, including working with others in a team setting – and they help when there is stuff we may not like doing - like tax returns – that have to be done by a deadline. These tools and skill-sets had to be built as part of the development of our economy. Mass production depends on dividing tasks into sub-tasks that can be repeated by many operatives at the same time. To succeed it requires an organisational framework to make sure the optimum numbers of workers are employed for the correct time. The aim of these tools is to make sure everything that needs to be done is known, the order in which tasks need to be done is clear, and the interrelationships or dependencies between tasks is mapped out. They are non-judgemental: they do not care about what it is we are doing. They have nothing say about our happiness, ethics or well-being.

Happiness is an elusive actor on our world stage. If there really is a huge backlog of things to do and we don't know where to start, we are likely to suffer stress. No matter what arguments we use or who we try to blame we won't get out of this pressured cul-de-sac until something gives. Sometimes the thing that gives is our health. According to guidance published by the UK's National Institute for Health and Clinical Excellence (NICE) in 2009, one in six adults in the UK suffer depression at some point in their lives[75]. In 2005 an independent report in the US estimated that 5% of men and 11% of woman were taking antidepressants[76]. Managing time is a good idea simply to help keep all this at bay. There will be times when we are forced into doing things that we might find difficult, but the satisfaction of getting things done on time is priceless. Choosing how we spend our time and then achieving what we set out to do make sense. So what happens if we feel we can't do something?

What if our work is not providing what we want? What then?

Work is sold as something close to paid slavery, mostly drudgery, sometimes painful and often boring. No wonder then that we need all these tools. The picture is one of reluctant sulky people being dragged through a swamp infested with mosquitoes in the midday sun. But what if work was fulfilling, exciting, creative and part of us, that is: work was something we loved to do anyway, would it still be work? In this case what would be the point of achieving a *four hour working week* as Tim Ferris suggests[77] in his book of the same name? His formula is to develop a sustainable income from products that others sell, for example an income based on royalties from the sale of a book – then pull the shade over, put your feet up and order another martini. If work is becoming more interesting, perhaps because the components of work are now beginning to include more creativity, then our perception of work and time may well change. Time spent being creative is very different from time spent on less engaging tasks.

How many of us have experienced creative flow[78]? Most of us at some point in our lives have been involved in something where time just doesn't matter – it flies by and nothing can interrupt us, because we are consumed by the task. Maybe the last time was at kindergarten but it probably has happened. What does this mean for our time managed lives?

A time-constrained life is not conducive to creativity. Once we achieve a sense of 'flow' we are compelled to stick with the task, we are drawn into it. There are no boundaries – the end of the task is the only deadline, and when that occurs can be very fluid. To illustrate the point let us contrast two activities. One involves completing a test of a piece of software, the other involves the design of a radical and novel transportation device that uses the properties of electromagnetism to provide levitation and propulsion. They are clearly very different. We would expect the software team to be working to a fixed deadline to ensure the product was working to a tightly controlled specification. We would expect the second task to be more open-ended. The engineers would be trying various ideas before finding the right solution. A third task may involve a much less defined problem, or perhaps be purely explorative, perhaps looking at the interface between organic and digital matter. This project may have no defined deadline at all. In her new book, *The Progress Principle*[79], Teresa Amabile explains how overtly structured project management and insensitive employee relations can damage progress on many levels and in particular, progress on tasks that include creativity. Instead, she recommends that the appropriate management must be applied and two main principles should always be followed: Firstly there need to be events that act as catalysts. These events should directly facilitate project work, such as setting clear goals and providing autonomy. Secondly there should be events that nourish interpersonal relationships. These events should uplift workers, provide encouragement and evidence of respect and collegiality. Fixed deadlines and pressurised time monitoring of performance do not sit well in a contemporary working environment.

Stepping out of this corporate world into the creative sphere, we can take away some interesting thoughts. In its raw form the traditional corporate time management machinery such as clocking in and out is unlikely to work. If it's creativity that we need then some unconstrained time must be allowed. This of course is an anathema to the mass production model but it is more in tune with quasi-creative companies that rely on both formal skills and creativity to deliver their products and services. When it comes to time management in the modern world some new thinking is needed.

As individuals possibly struggling to manage the demands on our time, we may well be experiencing more pressure to follow the formal time management mantra. The effect of this may well compress any time we may wish to devote to our creative capabilities whether as an entrepreneur, employee or as a leisure pursuit. According to iStock by Getty Images' first ever 'Free the Creative' survey[80] of more than 400 creative professionals in the USA and UK, nearly half of them believe that creativity is stagnating or declining in their profession due to tighter budgets, less time devoted to creativity and more time devoted to admin, meetings, and form filling. A quarter of respondents spent less than two hours a day being creative as a part of their job. They gave the view that if creatives had fewer priorities they would be twice as inspired at work. This is verified by Amebile's study, Creativity Under The Gun[81], which found that people were least creative when they were fighting the clock – and that when people are working under great pressure, their creativity reduces not only on that day but the next two as well.

There are occasions when working under a time constraint delivers a new creative insight, but most invention and innovation comes out of long term experimentation, where people are given time to explore.

Perfection

The Pareto law, otherwise known as the 80-20 rule, is used in commercial business to drive change and improvement. So statements such as 80% of profits are derived from 20% of customers, or 80% of your profits come from 20% of the time you spend, are used to justify changes that attempt to minimise costs and maximise profits. It is also used to explain why 80% of a project's value is gained by expending 20% of the resources needed. It is sometimes summarised as 'perfection is the enemy of the good'. For example Microsoft worked out that if they fixed the top 20% of bugs they would eliminate 80% of crashes and errors[82].

This is a reason why version 1 of a product may contain a small percentage of the full specification, which may not turn up until version 10. It doesn't have to be perfect to gain 80% of the target market. Does this thinking apply to creativity? By definition it is more difficult to apply. Creative outcomes often need to be 100%, or the best they can be, particularly if the creator's reputation and career is at stake. For example even if the budget is under pressure somehow the film still needs to be made with minimal creative compromises. A film within budget, but which has little artistic merit is unlikely to succeed. An over-budget movie that has an appeal due to its creative input is more likely to succeed. Of course an ideal is to have both budget control and creative excellence.

These opposing viewpoints may appear bizarre to those working in each sector. In the creative sector it may seem crazy to produce a 'sub standard product' and those who are used to markets for consumer goods may recall in horror at the needless quest for perfection. Both approaches seem correct to their protagonists. When the two collaborate, as occurs when large feature films are made, or advertising campaigns are mounted, the creative approach to time management is likely to bump into corporate funding constraints. A new way of managing is needed.

This demonstrates in part why tensions exist between these sectors. How time gets used and what expectations each group have of each other can lead to problems due to underlying different world views. The scripts that are running inside our minds about the way time should be used cause us to reject collaboration with those who do not comply. We develop these myths because we do not understand the needs of the other group.

Procrastination

Postponing important things because they are unpleasant or difficult? Well no one is perfect; avoiding difficult tasks is natural. It explains a lot about failure though - that somehow these things will all go away is a premier league myth; there is no easy way out. Hence no matter where we sit, in a studio with a graphic workstation wrestling with a Photoshop project, or in the finance department trying to deal with expense claims, the best way is to prioritise and get it done. Putting the difficult first is not a bad idea; somehow the longer 'difficult' stays on the to-do pile the more 'difficult' it gets. To be creative we need time to let our minds stray from the immediate to the imaginary, so having half of our minds occupied with a nagging task isn't going to help. Equally, putting off the one task that requires deep thought by shoving all the small admin tasks to the top of the list won't wash either; if we are working to a plan, we should stick to it. If our plan says spend all day in the studio, that's where we should be. If it says complete tax returns, then get it done.

Of course we all enjoy being creative. Being effective though requires a balance, once we have used our creativity to develop our ideas then more work is usually needed to harvest the fruits of our thinking, and this work often involves our logical selves. Our ideas may need to be tested; peer group reviews may be needed, as happens in the world of academia. If publishing is required we will need to sit down and explain our ideas. Time will need to be allocated to these tasks as well; planning in advance sensitises us to the work that needs to be done. That way it loses its emotional charge and it has less power to annoy us because we know about it, and we have allocated time to it.

If we don't plan this usually means we have a non-plan. Non-plans are plans in another guise; they are plans that will lead to failure. Instead of us controlling our time, now the non-plan controls our time and begins to take on the role of monster. Tasks begin to appear as if a devil is orchestrating our lives, our creative output is forever lost as one task after another demands our attention. To get through we must cut corners, and the quality of our professional relationships begin to suffer, as does the quality of our work. We find we are asked to rework time and again. Despite the allure of the addictive adrenaline-driven 'working up to the wire' deadline favoured by many, Non-plans are deadly.

Winging it

A lack of time and interest can mean we try to get through meetings, deal with people and institutions in a cursory way, making do with a minimum effort and hoping no-one notices. It is impossible to create a professional relationship by 'winging it'. That is: not giving enough time to preparation and research. Another common myth that 'I'm good at winging it' is a contradiction. Everyone else will agree, but what they see is an unreliable maverick who cannot be trusted. No-shows, being late and being unprepared are disrespectful and a pain in the ass. One way to enhance a career in any business? Turn up on time and know your stuff.

Time has a convoluted relationship with quality. Somewhere in there is a balancing act, where our qualities need to be exposed while time is ticking away. We could spend our whole lives perfecting what we want to offer the world, but never engaging with it, or we could strike out too early and find the world is expecting much more of us. Finding the balance is what our logical mind skills are for; part of achieving this balance is to appreciate how good we are at judging when the time is right.

Drummer wanted – no timewasters

This advert was commonplace in the 1960s and 70s. It implied that somehow a musician would know if they were a timewaster or not. What it meant was 'serious applicants only'. It didn't mean only 'good drummers' or only drummers that can keep time. Why? Well there were a lot of wannabes in music at that time. These are people who want the fame but are not prepared to do the work: they were not wanted at an audition for a serious artist. Wasting others' time or even our own time is a serious mistake. We may think that whatever we do doesn't matter because it is our time to do it in, given that everyone's time is limited, but unless we have discovered the elixir of life every moment of everybody's life is precious. Therefore the best use of our time and everyone else's is doing the things that we really want to do.

Sleep

Working 9 to 5 is a cliché. The world of business revolves around this roughly drawn sketch of how people work, that millions of people make the journey to work every day and fit regular sleep into their work patterns. This of course is a stereotype, but not without truth. Why would anyone want to break out of this routine? Creativity does not adhere to these types of constraint. Clearly there are physical benefits: regular eating and resting periods for example, but if creativity is to become a larger part of our working lives another way will need to be found to accommodate our work patterns. When we are being creative, work patterns can be erratic. Driven by the subject, and enjoying what we do, working on project after project, our sleep patterns represent a different perspective; they can get in the way. The myth that we should have regular work and rest patterns is a reflection of an old order, as we become increasingly connected and business spreads around the world how will we divide our time to satisfy the new demands for creativity and effectiveness?

Global awakening

Time zones calibrate our world; in the USA alone there are four different time zones. What time it is in New York will affect what can be done in other parts of the world. Stock markets trade around the globe 24 hours a day, as one closes another opens. We are all drawn into this sleepless world, through media, our work and our relationships. How we manage our time is changing, it may go through a chaotic phase, but a new equilibrium is required, one that respects our creativity and our rationality.

The tightrope walker

Somewhere along the line a balance has to be struck. Way out on the right is a consummate creative person, awash with thoughts, who can barely find time to change their socks. Out on the left is someone with a stopwatch gazing at spreadsheets. For most of us living around the centre of the bell curve we need to find time for both ways of life.

Part 3: Chapter 11: The bureaucracy myth

'Every revolution evaporates and leaves behind only the slime of a new bureaucracy.'

- Franz Kafka 1883-1924

Dealing with the machine

What has bureaucracy got to do with our logical and creative abilities?

If anything represents the footprint of logic rather than creativity, bureaucracy must step into the spotlight and take a bow. Ask the question: bureaucracy, what is it good for? And the reply would be tuneful if not polite. There are complaints that bureaucracy gets in the way of creativity, that it is designed for other types of people, that it is impossible to deal with, that bêtes noires such as forms, whether paper or digital, are too complex and too detailed and the associated deadlines impossible to meet. It is also cited as the reason for failure, for example to obtain funding for a project, or to avoid heavy penalties for late filing. Whilst there are many aspects of bureaucracy that challenge all of us, a deeper understanding of its role in our lives may help to explain why we've developed it, and despite its bad press, why it is useful.

Of relevance to our western civilisation, the *Leviathan*, a work of political philosophy written by Thomas Hobbes in 1651, embodies the fundamentals of our democratic and legal system, giving a green light to government by a body of elected individuals rather than by birthright. Followed by John Lock's treatises (1689) that underpinned the democratic development of the United States, the liberalist society that the West has come to represent was born. Once those principles were established, some way of enforcing these new rules and laws was needed. Institutions were developed to nurture the new democracy, and these were granted powers to intercede on behalf of all citizens to ensure fairness, sustainability and compliance. The liberalisation that had begun with the enlightenment and the scientific revolution began to form into workable systems in Europe and the New World. As imperfect as all this was, the fact that today we can point to previously unknown levels of wealth and freedom for many is a testament to the success of these institutions or to label them in our currency: bureaucracies.

Bureaucracy does have an impact on the way we live our lives and the progress we aim to make. We would expect this to be true, after all bureaucracies are set up to by us to provide the things we need; health care, education, water, electricity and law. They protect us from the stuff we don't want: crime, disease, poverty, starvation, homelessness and so on. We would soon complain if these protective sustaining services were taken away. However, the rules and procedures that help a bureaucracy to function can get in the way of progress and creative thought. Conflicts can arise between bureaucratic and creative environments, new ideas may flourish, and then simply be drowned by a tangled mesh of rules and procedures. Also these procedures can eat up the time available to think, making the working day seem soulless and boring, or causing interventions when we wish to concentrate on other tasks. Bureaucracies have a seemingly insatiable appetite, requiring us to complete forms and provide information so that decisions can be made, and we all have to deal with them. Perhaps the most severe accusation aimed at bureaucracies is cultural: they promote a 'can't do' mentality, every reason to change something can be countered by a rule that explains why it breaks a regulation or practice.

Bureaucracy seems to be the bogeyman on everyone's list. Associated with red tape and officialdom, it presents images of emotionless automatons wielding power from behind rows of desks, working systems of permissions and form-filling that are designed to thwart us all in our endeavours. Terry Gilliam's depiction of the state run for the preservation of the bureaucracy in the film 'Brazil'[83], feels accurate and unnerving although more whimsical than George Orwell's darkly pessimistic book '1984'[84]. The reality is that it's hard keeping track of people and what they want or need over a lifetime, and the more of us there are the more complex it all gets. Think about health records, births and deaths, marriages and pensions; we might not like all the form filling and record keeping but we'll appreciate it if we are ill, or want to register a new birth or inherit the family pile. Max Weber, the eminent sociologist and political economist, developed models of efficient bureaucracy and recognised that these systems were driven by the need to manage money and people. This of course brings power and influence, and the potential for corruption. The rule based bureaucracy, constructed to oversee fairness and equality, was in Weber's view the perfect foil for the 'barbarous behaviour' that characterised early 19th century organisations. Designed well, a modern bureaucracy should be transparent and supportive of the consensus reflected in the political structure; all very well when liberalism is the aim, but less enticing when repression is afoot. Bureaucracies are successful in their own terms, outliving many institutional changes and the merry-go- round of governments. In Weber's view the reason bureaucracies thrive is because 'there isn't a better way of doing things'[85].

So like it or not we're stuck with them; better then to learn how to deal with them, and to do that our logical selves stand ready. Bureaucracy can be viewed as a negative but necessary part of managing our world populations. The interface between us and 'it' often manifests as a 'form', either on paper or these days online as part of a website, that requires intellectual effort to complete. The data collected is sent to the relevant body that is invariably organised as a rule based hierarchy - and our 'case' can escalate or decant. The purpose of this data collection exercise is to provide the decision makers or bureaucrats with the details required to help them assess our case/ bid/request and then inform us of the outcome. For example we will complete forms when applying for planning permission to alter a house, or when applying for a driving licence.

We all have a citizen's responsibility to play this game. Behaving as if it doesn't matter will only lead to more bureaucracy, and sometimes very heavy-handed bureaucracy at that; in most countries of the world driving a car without a licence is a criminal offence. Complaining about bureaucracy does have some merit, but complying with it and moving on also has positive attractions. As we're all in the same boat, adults who cannot or will not complete forms are not generally respected by their peers unless there are mitigating circumstances; a mental disability for example. Those who refuse to complete forms may achieve some brief notoriety, but usually someone else is cleaning up their mess. So unless it is really obtuse or implies a breach of our security or privacy, filling in forms is an obligation we all have to deal with. That doesn't mean it is always a piece of cake; the UK social security regulations are now so complex that applicants need specialist help to find their way through the multitude of options and rules. In the US over 500 variants of personal tax forms exist, for many US citizens, employing an accountant is the only safe way of completing an end of year return.

Do lunch

Does our experience affect our ability to deal with bureaucracy? familiarisation with the workings of any bureaucracy will help. Having no exposure to form filling would be a disadvantage, however there are very few of us who would qualify as complete novices. Form filling begins during education and soon becomes a part of all our lives. For most of us, whether we have a creative or non-creative background, dealing with bureaucracy is a necessity and something we are all capable of managing. Form filling, decision making and meetings may be a poor bedfellows for creative work, draining away precious time and energy, but postponing or avoiding these tasks is also a risky exercise, leading to constant nagging, re-working and potentially incurring escalating penalties from within the bureaucracy. To be optimally productive during periods of creative flow requires zero distractions, even if the admin task is sitting on a to-do list the fact that it's now due will disrupt the most energised thoughts. We need to get to a point where meeting the demands of a bureaucracy is no more painful than doing lunch, schedule it away from the main activity of the day and make sure we get what we want.

We have a choice when dealing with bureaucracy. We can be good at it or we can suck at it. Our logical admin skills are of most use when trying to manage these types of tasks, having a balanced logical and creative mind means we should all be able to cope. If we delete the logical set, lobotomise our natural ability, then suddenly these activities become a problem. So we can refuse to fill in our tax forms, or fill them in inaccurately, we can forget to pay our bills, forget to register our kids for school or ignore the need for health care. The consequences are likely to be prosecution, or a high tax bill. Some level of skill at managing the bureaucracy is needed, and it's not as hard as it seems.

Please go away

All great civilisations have employed forms of bureaucracies to build and maintain their systems. Libraries, hospitals, universities, transportation, defence and so on are all examples that can be found in the Roman Empire, the Ming Dynasty, and The Ottoman Empire as well as in the West. Organising millions of people successfully can't be done on an ad-hoc day by day basis. Long term planning requires documentation, records, decisions, ideas and hard work. Think of the amount of information needed to plan a new road, and the numbers of organisations and people involved. Think about one of the most important landmarks of western civilisation, *The European Convention on Human Rights*[86] and how long it has taken to agree and implement this (it was first proposed in 1950 and ratified in 1953). Bureaucracies aren't about to stop or become less intrusive; what they all do is maintain our lives while attempting to get better at how they do this. We don't need to be afraid of them, we invented them, they are part of us.

Polishing the brass

Ideally a bureaucracy should be constantly reviewed and improved, which includes redesigning it if it doesn't work efficiently or is inordinately expensive. Examples of recent improvements are the plethora of self-completion forms on the websites of many government departments and most energy providers. This has reduced costs and improved accuracy of the data collected. It is now easier to interface with the machinery of government and other organisations. Not only have the costs been reduced but forms have been redesigned to be more understandable, and computer help scripts written to guide users through the process. It is now possible to complete standard tax returns using low cost computer tools, without talking to anyone in the revenue service.

Bureaucracies are intended to serve all their citizens and in the best cases should be politically neutral and transparent. There is nothing intrinsically evil about them although they wield power. Power can be used to gain advantages or to persecute. It is our use of bureaucracies that determines their behaviour. Claiming that they can't be dealt with or claiming that it is the reason for failure is a poor excuse. But lots of people do.

Yeah that's all very well but...

Sue writes: A friend of mine is a photographer, raconteur and generally fun bloke to be with. He makes his living by selling his photos, helping out with shows and making the odd appearance on stage. His view of dealing with tax returns is something akin to having root canal treatment. No amount of cajoling will convince him it is a relatively easy process these days, he has made it a part of a world he refuses to understand or be a part of. He considers those who inhabit this world to be 'prats'. So every year he postpones his tax return until the last minute, making his life a misery as the deadline approaches and the threat of a heavy fine looms over him. He is not alone among the creative community.

The point is that most of these creative people are highly intelligent, but are being floored by something that people who work in the conventional business world view as no more complex than an elementary school test.

To be fair, a creative person's work culture is ideally very non-bureaucratic, the fact that they are being required to deal with work in this way can cause frustration and annoyance. For example tensions exist between the creative and back office staff within organisations such as advertising companies. This can lead to emotionally charged arguments. Getting in touch with our logical side is a way out, and something we can all do even if it doesn't fit in with the way we think and organise ourselves in our mainstream job.

Where's the money

Another consequence of a 'pure' creative lifestyle that rejects the need to be logical from time to time, is the failure to secure grants. There are many artists who complain that they are never given anything and many who don't apply because it's too difficult. The writing of bids and pitches requires careful thought, even if the intention is to use crowd funding rather than single funding support. The funders often have strict conditions that need to be met. Filling in the forms precisely and gathering the right evidence is just as important as the proposed art form or performance. Not everyone gets this.

Working the magic

Mike writes: In 2006 The Jamestown Union, a local Indie rock band in Brighton, UK had been selected to play at two prestigious international music festivals, one in Houston, Texas the other in Toronto. The band were just starting out, they'd made their debut album at their own expense, a mix of local feelings with an 'Americana' sound, pretty cool stuff, guitar, drums, bass, mandolin, pedal steel, banjo with a charismatic, photogenic lead singer. They had some reviews and a local following that showed they were going places. The cost of getting to these festivals ran into the thousands of pounds, money the band didn't have. For the Houston gig the band applied to Arts Council England (ACE) for support. The local regional office had a scheme that provided funding support for local arts projects including music, particularly if there was an international dimension. The detail required on the application form needed to show why any grant would fit with ACE objectives for promoting UK arts abroad. This meant there had to be a UK angle, something that played to the reputation of UK arts, would improve the standing of UK arts abroad, and would reach a lot of people. The festival boasted a potential ticket sale of 30,000+ music fans. The band was the only UK act selected for the festival. The case for the grant was based on the uniqueness of the opportunity, the fact that the band had a new album to promote, and that the festival provided a way to connect with new fans in the US, and fly the flag for UK arts. The band called before submitting their grant application to check what was required. They were advised to include a detailed budget that showed an equal contribution towards the costs from other parties, and show how the money was to be spent. A detailed plan was also required – basically a schedule of events the band would be involved in – things like promotion meetings and networking opportunities, as well as live performances. This included help from the UK department of trade and industry who were able to put the band in contact with US agents. The application form was submitted. There were a few points that needed clarification so a second round of amendments went in. The band got a grant of £2,500 towards the trip costs.

For the second festival, *North by North East* (NXNE) in Toronto, the band was directed to a different funding organisation: UK Music Abroad. ACE had changed their funding policy and now contributed donor grant funds to this organisation and then left them to distribute the money. Other donor sources of funding, including the Performing Rights Society (PRS), contributed to provide over £1 million in funds to support UK music abroad. The band made their application assuming similar details were expected. In this case the funder also requested a copy of the debut album. As the festival date approached the band had heard nothing from the funders. A call was made. They were told their application had been rejected. The reasons given were that the application wasn't convincing. What 'PRS for Music' were looking for was a list of music industry contacts that were set up in Toronto in advance of the festival, a supporting record label or a management company, and a band biography that suggested the band were serious. They were not interested in the UK angle, budgets, or detailed plans. Lesson 1: check out what the funders want, on the phone, before applying and forget any assumptions from previous experiences.

The story doesn't end there. In Brighton, the band's home town, a local music festival *The Great Escape* took place the same week the band heard about the grant refusal. At the festival, UK Music Abroad and ACE were part of a panel that dealt with getting funding support to help musicians and bands selected for festivals abroad. They gave their presentation about how they could help for festivals like NXNE and the prestigious South By South West (SXSW). At the end of the presentation the band stood up and asked the panel what they should do, as they had been offered a place at NXNE. The panel said 'apply for our grant!' The panel looked dumbfounded when the band said they had, and it had been turned down. The next day the band got a call, asking them to resubmit their application.

They were given instructions on what to include and what the funders were looking for. The application was rewritten. Now it included the promotions company in Canada, the supporting management company in the UK, the label meetings that had been set up, a band biog that showed how the band aimed to grow their fan base and how they were going to sell their music in the North American market. A few days later they were told the grant had been approved - £2,000. Lesson 2: don't give up.

The band went on to play at NXNE, got invited back to Canadian Music Week the following year, again with PRS for Music support. The band were also invited to NXNE for a second year, and were scheduled to apply for (SXSW) – the next step. By this time the band were confident they could get grant support if they needed it. The bureaucracy was no longer difficult, it was beneficial. Their experience had honed the band's ability to get help from places that seemed impenetrable but in reality were on their side. Lesson 3: don't be afraid to ask.

After both festivals the band wrote up how they'd benefited, who they'd met and what they were planning next, as well as putting up videos and stories of the trip on their website. These reports were sent to the funders. That meant next time they needed support they could prove that the money was well spent, and it had been used for the intended purpose. Lesson 4: keep them involved and let them know about any success.

But that's not the whole story. The first festival in Houston was cancelled at the last minute because of poor ticket sales and bad weather. The band found out on their way to the airport. The grant money is only paid after the festival not before, and requires evidence before it's paid. After a lot of soul searching they decided not to go. They lost the money for the airfares and the hotels, however one of the band went anyway. He'd decided to get to Nashville and take the album round to the music labels. He arrived in Houston in the middle of a snow storm, got a bus to the city centre and found a cheap hotel, popular with drunks and junkies. The next day he took a bus to Nashville. Just outside Memphis the bus crashed, having skidded on the icy roads; he was ok but shaken up. The bus was on its side. He called a cab from Memphis and got to the hotel, where he bumped into an old friend from Brighton UK. He stayed in Memphis for a day to recuperate then took the final leg of the bus ride up to Nashville. In Nashville it was so cold the ATMs were frozen! He was out of money but managed to get a hotel which the band paid for over the internet. He got to see several labels over the next few days, and although no-one offered the band that all important 'deal' he made a lot of contacts. Finally he made his way back down to Houston and flew home. The band told ACE the whole story. ACE gave the band 50% of the grant in recognition of their honesty, and the fact they did all they could. Their view was that in the arts sector, these things happen. Lesson 5: be honest.

Making the impossible possible

The language and behaviour inside a bureaucracy can be resistant to any form of change. Evaluation is a trait of such organisations, a consequence of their role as decision makers, and it is easy for a culture of fault finding to take root. Breaking out of this requires self awareness and help from those who can infuse a different mind set. If these organisations are to become more creative, then their default communications style needs to change. Open dialogue as discussed in Linda Ellinor and Glenna Gerard's book, *Dialogue: Rediscover the Transforming Power of Conversation*[87], can begin to loosen the relationships within a bureaucracy and kick-start new ideas. Getting rid of the formal structure aligned through departments can also help, replacing this with project working, but more on this in later chapters. Making sure we don't turn into stone statues as a result of our tangle with bureaucracy is one thing we all need to be aware of, and one way to deal with it is to keep one step ahead. What can help is training and mentoring.

Self development

This is a good thing. Anyone disagree? Well if you work in the creative sector you might. The Creative Industries Business Advisory Service (CIBAS) is based in Portsmouth, a large UK city, and their brief is to help creative entrepreneurs become financially viable. They often hold evening events to celebrate their achievements. At one such event they invited a keynote speaker, who had been on the TV programme 'Dragons Den', to open the event, to be followed by three local speakers.

The speaker was a creative entrepreneur. Her story began while she had been on a holiday, and wanted to help a local African tribe to sell their jewellery. So she set up a small company to do that. Then she realised that there were no suitable boxes to put the jewellery in, so she set up the 'Small Box Company'. This became very successful, and still is.

The second speaker came on stage very tentatively. She was a weaver, and told the audience how CIBAS had helped her by always being at the end of a phone when she was feeling that nobody liked her work, and how they would calm her down and advise her to have a nice cup of camomile tea. The help and advice she sought was not about spreadsheets and business plans, because her main goals weren't about money. Does it count if someone isn't actually all that bothered about making money?

CIBAS would often trick their clients into receiving help. If they sent out an invitation to a 'Creative Industry networking event' , no-one would come, but if they quietly said to a textile artist 'come along tomorrow afternoon and I can sit you next to the buyer from Liberty's' , they would come.

Our research, conducted among a group of creative practitioners was enlightening. They were asked how likely they would be to attend a training course aimed at improving their business skills. They were given four scenarios, each one requiring differing levels of cost. 1. The course involved a small cost, 2. Free, 3. Expenses would be paid, 4. Expenses were covered and paid to attend. The responses were: 13% would attend if they had to pay a small fee. 48% if the course was free. 73% if expenses were paid, and 97% if expenses and payments were made. 3% would not attend even if they were paid. This contrasts with courses aimed at improving their creative skill which they would all have paid for. The difficulty of engaging them in the business of business seems related to the value they place on such knowledge. In his book entitled *Creativity* Mihaly Czsikszentmihali documents the lives of 400 notable creative artists, business leaders, scientists and writers. He discovered that they all found sanctuary in their work from 'the noise of normal life' with its distractions and constant interventions. Within this sheltered world, the issues of managing day to day matters were ignored, no matter how important they may seem to others, and quite rightly so, so long as it is for a defined period of time when they were in 'Flow'. It is impossible to be uniquely creative or concentrate on one topic for extended periods if you are being asked to deal with multiple tasks at the same time. The true value of their lives lay in their dedication to their subject. No wonder then that it is difficult to engage such people in training that ostensibly seems to bear no connection to the task at hand. The approach taken by CIBAS – to disguise such training as being related to the main creative activity in some way, and avoiding stock managerial terms would seem to be an effective way of building trust and adding value.

Keeping up

Bureaucracy may make a good scapegoat when we need an excuse for why things have gone wrong. We can acknowledge that organisations are not perfect, and that the way they work is sometimes the opposite of our ideal. Still the point must remain that bureaucracy is 'the best way of doing things'. The interface between us and bureaucracy is becoming much easier to use, and most tasks are not intellectually challenging. For short periods in our lives we need to be organised enough to deal with our responsibilities and that requires our logical and rational capabilities to step forward. The classic bureaucracy is changing, not as fast as the commercial organisations that rely on it, but it too will need to embrace creative working and new ideas. The people who will come to work in these bureaucracies will need to utilise their creative as well as logical skills. The new game in town is not factory work, it is knowledge work.

Bureaucracy may be appear to be an unthinking machine, but it's a machine that is not going away. It's not hard to deal with and once mastered our lives can get easier. The revolution lies elsewhere.

Part 3: Chapter 12: Endemic or pandemic?

'Fear and euphoria are dominant forces, and fear is many multiples the size of euphoria. Bubbles go up very slowly as euphoria builds. Then fear hits, and it comes down very sharply. When I started to look at that, I was sort of intellectually shocked. Contagion is the critical phenomenon which causes the thing to fall apart'.

- Alan Greenspan

The international perspective

Does the lobotomy affect the whole world in the same way? This book has been focussing on western societies, where 19th century industrialisation has left its mark on people, policies and systems. But other societies have a markedly different approach to creativity and may not have experienced the same industrialisation process. In short they may have the hallmarks of the lobotomy but may not be experiencing its symptoms, in other words they may have become industrialised but not in the same way. There may be some underlying cultural differences such as how creativity is understood or how creativity is embedded within a culture. The nature of creativity may be extrinsic, rather than intrinsic - an external muse or spirit providing the source of inspiration, not an internal section of the brain. This may give the impression that creativity is undervalued in the west, i.e. seen as functional and mechanical rather than spiritual and holistically human. However it can be argued that it is simply valued differently, and is also developed in a different way. So to illustrate: Picture two people grappling with a demanding problem. One may be waiting for inspiration from the muse (an eastern approach), the other is using skills and techniques as part of their 'creative muscle' (the western approach). The latter could be said to be more successful as evidenced by the major innovations produced by the West in the last 500 years. When we use our creativity in harmony with our logic then optimal results can be expected, and the more we practise the better these results can be. If we divide these two capabilities and start forcing people to make choices about how they think, the results get worse.

The division of creativity and logic into sub-culture policy and work practice may not have happened in other cultures, or may be happening in different ways. Certainly for those countries that are experiencing transitions to modern industrial economies there may be dangers, and there may be indicators that similar destructive forces are at play. If such a gap has been identified, perhaps as a factor of innovation capability, are they closing the gap, or approaching the reconciliation in a different way? Or maybe they always had both creativity and logical business methods embedded within their working practices and never got rid of creativity in the workplace? Famously the Japanese *Kaizen* system, which broadly means giving responsibility to the workforce to improve products and production, led to the startling success of their car industry, and the development of their electronics industry.

Is the prejudice less pronounced in countries that do not pursue the western model and viewpoint? If they view creativity differently and as less elitist, or more as a spiritual and shared attribute that is not attached to an individual, do they still encounter this divorce between the creatives and those working in conventional business environments?

Globally speaking, most Governments say they encourage creativity, but their actions may belie their words; many political structures are sustained by ignorance. In autocracies, education and especially creative thinkers pose perhaps the greatest threat to their existence. Indeed, due to the ignorance and narrow-mindedness of a large proportion of the electorate, the level of political discourse in many of the world's so-called democracies is only slightly above that of the autocracies, if it is above that level at all.

Does this mean that democracies are better at fusing creativity and business then, and that the gap is narrower? Certainly a democratic model, for either a government or a business or a relationship, with a 'flat hierarchy' or at least one where the views and ideas of everyone are given a voice and are held in high esteem, rather than just a ruling elite, is one that seems to narrow the gap.

In any one culture there is generally an agreement over what is accepted as creative, but cultures differ in their thinking – there are ethnic differences, especially between Asians and Westerners, who exhibit different perceptual and cognitive processes. While the Western idea of creativity is *revolutionary,* the Asian cultures favour an *evolutionary* view. Western cultures have recognised creativity most in the service of human needs, largely in a materialistic sense. This has led to an emphasis on a product-orientated approach. It is therefore not surprising to find the qualities of novelty and functionality as critical to the identification of creativity. This, however is not the idea of creativity in other cultural traditions. The Asians, particularly the Chinese, are holistic. They look at the big picture and attach causality to it, and make limited use of formal logic, whereas Westerners are more analytic, pay attention to objects and categories to which things belong and use formal logic to understand behaviour.

India, more than any other cultural region, offers a pluralistic vision of knowledge. With its systems of thought such as Vedic, Samkhya, Yoga, Vedant, Buddhist, Jain and the like it understands a diversity in viewing reality. The Indian mind accepts the possibility of more than one path to truth. The western perspective on artistic achievement is vertical, (towards one area in depth), eastern is horizontal (allows several domains to mingle with each other and synthesise into a new being).

Historical perspective

The ancient Greeks believed that the gods or the muses (the nine daughters of Zeus who ruled over the arts and sciences) breathed creative ideas into the artist, who called on them for inspiration for creative work and ideas. This idea is advanced with the commonly held belief that the unconscious mind presents the conscious mind with ideas, making the assumption that we make a creative leap without knowing how it came about.

An example would be Mozart as portrayed in Peter Shaffer's film 'Amadeus'; a vulgar, immature man who is constantly drunk and in debt, and yet who produces wonderful music without thinking about it – when the time is right, the music starts to flow, and Mozart simply writes it down. (Coincidentally, this film was often shown to music GCSE classes at a school where Sue used to work, and it was noted that 'if you were Mozart, you wouldn't get your GCSE' – primarily because a high percentage of marks at GCSE level are given to the evaluative or process phase of creativity (as defined by the National Advisory Committee on Creative and Cultural Education chaired by Sir Ken Robinson), and since Mozart's manuscripts show no evidence of deletions or corrections he would not have passed this component of the examination).

Conclusion

There are clear differences between East and West in the way creativity is understood and practised. In the East there is a closer alignment with spiritual inspiration as the source of creative activity (extrinsic stimulation), whereas the West sees creativity as an internal capability that can be developed, which explains in part the growth of Western science as well as the economic success achieved by mechanisation and industrialisation. However in terms of process of achievement there are similarities. The Eastern model of true knowledge is based on the same principles as that of Flow. That is:

not just being receptive to ideas (or allowing yourself to generate them) but also being disciplined and expert in the subject.

The Western model implies a capability that can be improved with practice, which depends on collaboration between creative work and logic, both key elements of the human brain. The gap undermines this Western model by breaking the link. The Eastern model is layered but has as its root an external creative stimulus making it much more difficult to introduce an over-emphasis on any one component. It may be that Eastern models of creativity are therefore more robust and valued and are less prone to invasion by overly logical ideas that could subvert productive behaviour and undermine collaborative relationships.

Part 4: Medications

Part 4: Chapter 13: Antidotes, solutions and cures

'I'm sick of being fucked about by men in suits sitting on their fat arses in the City'

- John Lennon, 1967

(Commenting on the takeover battle for Northern Songs, the company that owned the copyrights to the Beatles songs)

Having reached this part of the book we hope you will have recognised some of the symptoms of the lobotomy and have decided to do something about it. We'll suggest ways that can help to get your business side working or your creativity fired up. The aim is to help you get to better place. We've broken this chapter into three parts. First we'll look at self development - what can we do as individuals. Secondly we'll focus on organisations - what can we do to fix our workplaces. Finally we'll look at strategies for policy makers - making the world a better place for the longer term.

How big a change is made depends on where we're standing - maybe a small adjustment - a spoonful of sugar - or a major overhaul - a change of behaviour, attitude and lifestyle. In chapter four we intimated that a shift in attitude towards others, particularly if they work in areas that are different from our own, can dismantle some of the prejudices arising from the lobotomy. That's a good place to start.

Working as a creative person today usually means working as a freelancer. Not always true of course, for example creative thinkers are sometimes employed in staff teams by advertising companies. The team's daily grind is to come up with unique compelling campaign ideas that will excite the client and make us all rush to our computers to buy the product. However as we have seen in chapter five, the freelance model of operating in a loose network and picking up short term contracts is the common structure found in this market. Hours can be long, but the work is rewarding. On the other hand you may be in one of the more traditional work careers: the job is the same each day, hours are fixed and the tasks can be repetitive and mundane. Most of us are somewhere between these two scenarios and your needs may vary accordingly, but if you need to inject some creativity into your life or need to find a more sustainable lifestyle then hopefully the following will prove useful.

Before we begin it is worth saying that solutions to becoming more creative and/or wealthy are everywhere. You can find many books, courses and internet sites that suggest ways in which this can be achieved. Creativity has also become in many ways the number one fad, not only for personal development but also as part of a business strategy and a component of government policies and political party manifestos. If you've already found the holy grail and it works for you then great. But if you are treading water and it's getting deeper with no sight of a rescue boat then maybe our ideas will help you get to some higher ground. Firstly we will take a look at creativity.

Boosting creativity: The temple

Today experiments are being conducted to map creative activity using a brain scanner. This means sticking someone's head inside a machine which can detect changes in brain activity levels and code them as different colours. The result is red, blue, green and yellow blotches on a map of the skull. These are not much use unless these can be tied to creative activity, so the guinea pig is asked to think creatively while the machine whirs overhead. The resulting colour pictures identify different levels of activity in regions of the brain over intervals of microseconds. The hope is that some useful patterns can be identified that can lead to the development of an artificial stimulant for creativity. This stimulant might then be medicated through injection or encouraged through electrodes.

By its nature, creativity is unlikely to be improved either in quantity or quality just by trying to see where it is and then somehow increase it. Creativity is better understood as being made up of a collection of human abilities. There are a set of gold standard skills that have become associated with creativity; these can be thought of as the 'pillars of creativity'. They are very measurable, and can be improved, so we are going to start there.

The 12 primary pillars of creativity are: Confidence and self esteem, problem identification, problem solving, diverse thinking, collaboration, fascination, risk taking, gaining new skills, accepting challenges, developing new ideas, increased capacity to learn, and producing valued outcomes. Think of these as pillars that hold up the roof of a temple where your creativity can exist, and inside can be whatever is needed to help you be creative. Your temple can contain anything that you want that will help you. It will probably contain tools and ideas, your knowledge and experience and inputs from others. It can be a place of peace and contemplation, maybe without any external interference, but also maybe stimulated by it. Some abilities may depend on others: developing new ideas may depend on your appetite to gain new skills and apply problem solving. In this way we can start to see how creativity can be improved by upping levels in these measurable more tangible abilities.

This list of abilities provides a starting point, or a way in, which depends on what you want to achieve and where you are starting from. Once inside you can take on the many recommendations in self-help literature such as finding more time and space, thinking outside the box, dropping the dependence on email or social networks, reaching out to others, and so on. To begin you can decide which of these abilities you may need to work on first. For example if you decide that its new skills that you need to boost your creativity, then what skills? Once you've decided on that do you have the capacity to learn these new skills? Once you've committed to learning these new skills, do you need to collaborate with others? You are now taking new risks, and once these skills are acquired your confidence and self esteem will improve. How about identifying and solving problems? Again this profile of interventions may be the right fit for you. For someone else they may realise that they need to raise their game when it comes to problem identification and then perhaps become fascinated by a new challenge that requires problem solving skills. Instead of starting with a neutral action such as 'find more time' or 'go for a walk' it provides a structured way of finding a path to enhance creativity in any field of work.

It can be applied to you or to others; you may consider it useful for your children or your work colleagues to find the right direction and starting point.

So an example might be that you want to boost your creativity by becoming an artist who paints for pleasure. The outcome of your creativity-raising exercise will be the ability to paint the pictures you want and of course those pictures will represent that achievement. Where can you start? Drawing up a plan will help to get you through. Perhaps it is being reminded of the skill you had at school, or gaining completely new knowledge. At some point you will need to take new risks and meet new people, perhaps through a local education centre or through contacts at the art shop. Perhaps joining a group workshop will help. Collaboration is often an effective way to get from A to B quickly.

Another example may be that you wish to take on a new job, one that requires more responsibility and decision making. More and more employers are beginning to value creativity as a skill in their workforces. In this case developing problem identification skills, and problem solving strategies together with diverse thinking could raise your profile above that of the other candidates, and make you feel more confident.

Finally perhaps your children are finding school tough. Setting them some new challenges, finding new creative ways to look at the material they are learning, raising their engagement and encouraging fascination with their subjects as a result, may change their attitude, raise their self esteem and bring greater success.

Be mindful that being creative is a different experience from 'getting a job done'. Creativity calls on emotions and intuition as well as drawing on your skills and experience. Be aware that ideas can be deeply felt, and in their embryonic stage they can be fragile and easily destroyed. New ideas may require validation, and do require risk-taking on a personal level. It is not the same as taking a test. So be aware that the creative journey can take you to unexpected places, be confident but also accept setbacks. Realise that you will get there but that it will take time and patience.

Inside this imaginary temple is a place to build creativity. Once inside there are techniques that may help you to get started; we will look at some of these but this is not an exhaustive list; as we mentioned before there are many approaches.

Techniques to boost creativity

As Louis Pasteur once famously said, 'Chance favours only the prepared mind.' To maximise the benefits you need to foster creativity in your daily life so that your mind is ready when opportunity arises, so in short the regular use of these techniques will pay off.

Get out of the cage

Diverse thinking is an ability we are born with. It gets dulled over time as we focus on narrower skills that will become our mainstay career and if we take on jobs that demand less of our emotional playful side and more of our rational and logical capacities. To re-energise our diverse thinking we can use humour and fun. For example challenge yourself to come up with as many uses as you can of an object such as a paper clip or a brick, in five minutes. List them all and accept any idea as valid. This can also be done as a group exercise introducing an element of competition – who can think of the most in number, or the most bizarre? There is no need to evaluate these suggestions, as they are just fun. Try using different situations to stimulate the thinking. Situations such as sports activities, shopping, driving, relaxing on a beach or completing a DIY job may trigger a novel use of the object. Carrying out an exercise such as this regularly can help to broaden our world of possibilities, and revitalise our imagination.

A day out

Another technique that may help with problem solving is to take an imaginary excursion with someone who is recognised as a creative thinker. In this case ask the question 'what would this person do?' This could be a musician such as Madonna or Mick Jagger or perhaps a notable business person such as Richard Branson or a politician such as Hillary Clinton. These people are examples of those who do things differently. Allowing ourselves to be in their shoes can help us to come up with ideas we might otherwise not consider.

Step by step

Doing something outside your normal day to day life, something creative and non routine can be risky. What's at stake is your pride and confidence. So it is best to start small. Take on a low risk project first and have fun. It won't matter if it doesn't turn out perfectly. Trying stuff out and making mistakes is the best way to learn. Once you feel more confident then that may be the point to raise your game and start involving others and asking for feedback.

Polish and shine

You may hear phrases like 'perfection is the enemy of the good', or be given advice that 80% of any project's value is delivered by just 20% of the effort. When it comes to creativity this common business mantra about avoiding perfection does not apply. Most creative products need to be as good as they can be - there isn't an acceptable painting that can be 20% complete. It is also better to wait until you are satisfied with your creations before taking them out into the world. Only send out your best stuff.

Picture this

Use of metaphor is a natural way to explain our ideas to others and many of us fall into this mode of communication easily. It is useful to visualise metaphors to help our own understanding of new ideas. An example may be to think about a forthcoming business trip as a roller-coaster fairground ride, where dips and turns represent the ebb and flow of the arguments and discussions. Perhaps a simple problem such as how to clean windows in high rise buildings may be linked to a new use of car windscreen wiper technology.

Turn the clock around

Finding time is important. Sounds obvious but in this case it is essential to have lots of single task time, not multi-task time. If there is one major aspect of modern life that drains away creativity it is the lack of time. Creative activities are emotionally consuming (because we enjoy them so much) and time can appear to stand still, however the slightest interruption can dispel the mood and fracture our thought processes. Therefore it is a requirement to make time available when we are not thinking of anything else. How much time depends on you, but it must be zoned off.

Anywhere any place

Anywhere will do. Where you are when creative thoughts take place can be well… anywhere. Some find travelling on planes, trains and buses a good place to think, others need a home studio, others a library. There is no rule, just what suits you, and it can be all of these places. Allowing yourself to be creative will make the difference.

Bicycle balance

A useful way of thinking of our emotional-creative v logical-rational lives is to imagine we are riding a bicycle. The front wheel represents our creative ideas. The rear wheel represents what we do with them. Together they create a way through life. Both are needed. We could take this metaphor further by asking what happens when the balance is wrong. Riding a unicycle is tough, as is a penny farthing, but a tandem can be very productive – if the other person is pulling their weight.

As mentioned before there are many recommendations about ways in which creative stimulation can be started and nurtured. Many are reflections from individuals who work in creative jobs. As their approaches worked for them, there is a good chance they will work for you too, but they are based on unique experiences and environments and they may not be practical or appropriate to you and your situation. Some of these ideas are listed at the end of this chapter but an internet search will probably provide more than enough.

Boosting your business

So what can be done if creativity is already at the centre of your life but rewards are low and economic success seems a pipe-dream? That is you have a temple, you have ideas but you don't have money.
It is worth restating that the language, dress codes, work culture and

social interfaces in the creative industries are different from the more traditional work lifestyles. That doesn't mean they are on another planet. Perhaps the hardest point to overcome is that as a creative worker you are an entrepreneur, running a business, and in many cases that business is you. How you get rewarded is a business decision that you make.

Having said that, business has its own language and rules and it is largely a non-emotional place. It can seem like business is designed to kill creativity because it can be time consuming, obscure, seemingly just about money and often impossible to understand. However it can be simplified and once it is explained that's it. Or to put it more plainly, it is not like having to maintain the skills in your chosen creative area – photography, writing, art, computer games programming, website design etc. It is one body of knowledge that hardy ever changes and once it's learnt you're done.

Basically what needs to be learnt are the 'three M's': marketing, money and management.

Marketing: Work out who your customers are, where they are, then go and introduce yourself.
Money: Work out how much you need to make and how.
Management: Making sure you know where everything is and what other people should be doing for you.

Business flow

Think of business as a water wheel. Your work effort is represented by the water that arrives at the wheel. That effort is used to make products represented by the water held in the buckets of the wheel. As the buckets fill up the wheel turns and releases them into the market. Now imagine a second water wheel. In this case the water arriving represents the money arriving from sales of products, being used to pay you and your staff, and your bills. The excess then flows out to buy more raw materials. You'll need to keep a check on water flows to make sure you have enough to keep the business running and growing. Knowing how these wheels work will help you to keep track and find ways to do things like produce more for less.

This simple metaphor may help to open a way of thinking about business that helps to demystify it. Once the mechanism is understood then a business can be run while more products are developed. The tools we can use to develop this mechanism are easily available: spreadsheet software is enough to get us started. However we are not going to spend a lot of time explaining business tools here, there are many courses and websites that can do that. Some may suggest that it can be no different to deal with from any other aspect of a creative life – but we know that there are barriers.

For the solo creative

There is plenty of advice around for those involved in the world of business who would like to become more creative. But when it comes to creative people, there is not much help that is tailored towards those of us who want to access our logical side. The jobs and lives of creative people are often closely interwoven, and you may love what you do so much that it can be very difficult, and in some cases bordering on the offensive, for you to frame what you do as a business. It can feel very wrong to think of your artistic and creative practice in those terms and hard to make your life's passion fit into structures and terminology that have been created for the purposes of tracking and increasing financial profit. So we'd like to suggest that it might help if you can *pretend* that you are running a business – ask yourself ' if I *were* to be running a business, how would I do this?' Turn it into a game and use your creativity; that way you may avoid becoming entangled in your own prejudices and fears. Often the facts of what you need to do to run your business are there, but presented in a such a dull, impenetrable, opaque and generally rational way and that it's nigh on impossible for you to force – let alone motivate - yourself to actually do it. What follows is a list of tips and suggestions, in no particular order, which could help you to make better friends with your logical side.

File it

Creatives like to keep possibilities open. So when it comes to filing and tidying up, you may find yourself experiencing resistance due to the belief that once an item is filed and put away (either digitally or in the 'real' world), its purpose becomes fixed, and it's potential is lost to view. One thing that can help is to store things in clear transparent files and boxes, so they still remain visible. Clear box files and shoeboxes can be bought online. This can mitigate against the sense of rising panic that can occur when putting things away.

Tidy it

There are many decluttering systems and programmes out there. A particularly interesting one is 'The Life- Changing Magic of Tidying' by Marie Kondo (Vermilion, 2015). Her 'Konmarie method' involves collecting all the items you have in one group, shirts for example, then sitting quietly with each item in your arms in turn. If it sparks joy, you keep it. If not, you get rid of it. She advocates working through items in a particular order, and offers other useful tips such as suggesting that items that have sat at the back of a cupboard for over a year are feeling unloved – so motivating you emotionally to find a new home for them. She also advocates thanking your possessions for doing a good job on a regular basis. This personifying of objects can be very attractive to the creative mind, being amusing and engaging.

Plan it

As a freelance creative, you are running a business so you need to keep track, but the majority of planners and diaries out there are so dull that it can be a chore to open them. Look for inspiring and engaging ones that encourage you to express your ideas in creative ways. Leonie Dawson (www.leoniedawson.com) is a jolly Australian business guru who produces a range of planners and diaries with engaging prompts and use of colour, and www.dailygreatness.co publish an excellent planner which guides us to begin and end our day with clear intentions, a positive focused mindset and conscious reflection. These types of planner engage the creative mind by using compelling language and imagery. They urge you to set compelling and exciting goals, change your habits, examine your dreams and challenge your fears and understand that you learn best when you are playing. So this makes it easier for to create a productive daily routine.

See it

Draw up big wall charts and put them up on your wall so that they are immediately visible. This makes more sense to a visual creative mind rather than hiding schedules away on a spreadsheet. You can buy one and personalise it with colour and artwork, or create your own from scratch.

Let's work together

You may find it easier to work with others around you. Many cities have some form of co-working space, where you can work in the company of others. This can either be an arrangement where you pay a regular fee for your own space, or you can sometimes rent a hot desk on an hourly basis. Working in a café can also be beneficial – think about where you are most creative and productive and why, to help you decide if it is worth the investment to do this.

Let's network

There are a huge plethora of networking opportunities around. Some groups are costly to join, others are free – but all are of great benefit to creatives who work alone. Isolation is good when you need to be in flow, but can become unhealthy if it carries on too long – and of course you can run your ideas past other people or gain prospective clients when out networking.

Accountability buddy

If you have loads of creative ideas but you find it hard to motivate yourself to actually put these ideas into action, team up with someone else and call each other to task – agree set times to connect and go through each other's 'to do' list – it is often easier to get a task done if you know someone else is waiting and going to be calling you to account.

False deadlines

The stereotype of the creative procrastinating right up to just before the deadline, then completing the work in just a few hours whilst cursing themselves for not starting earlier. is alive and strong. Try to get round this by creating false deadlines for yourself – again, you can involve someone else by making a date for them to look at your work in advance of the 'real' deadline.

Tax lock-ins

Get together with a few other creatives and a tax advisor. You all chip in to pay the advisor, who is there on hand to answer any questions you have and also to make phone calls to the authorities on your behalf should you need it. This is a very effective way to reduce stress over tax issues or anything of a similar nature – get into the habit of paying for stuff that you're no good at or that stresses you out.

Self-confidence

It is quite common to have low confidence levels about our work – because there is often little division between our selves and our work. Getting on top the business side of your business will help to boost your confidence and vice-versa. Refer back to the work on the muse by Elizabeth Gilbert mentioned earlier in this book which offer the idea that rather than being a genius we all have a genius – take your 'self' out of the equation! Here's the link to the talk http://www.ted.com/talks/elizabeth_gilbert_on_genius?language=en

Affirmations

Authors such as Rhonda Byrne ('The Secret' www.thesecret.tv), Brené Brown (www.brenebrown.com/,) Byron Katie (www.thework.com/) and many titles published by the Hay House group come highly recommended and can help with feelings of vulnerability, shame and fear. Affirmations are highly recommended and can be added into your daily routine, prompted by your creative business planner as mentioned previously. One aspect that is often overlooked is fear of success - the flip side to fear of failure, this fear often needs work in creative people. Try the Emotional Freedom Technique (EFT) to banish these feelings.

Projects

We can treat this need to understand business just like a project to raise our creativity. This may appear slightly askew but indulge us. In this case new knowledge is needed: the knowledge of running a business, which once learnt should make more time available for our creative endeavours. We will have more confidence in our sales abilities which should lead to better returns. We will have more confidence that our money is under control and is well managed.

Somewhere down the line the business may become so successful that the associated admin tasks can be done by someone else. At that point you will have ridden the escalator to the next floor.

Next we're going to look at how creativity can be built into organisations.

Creativity within organisations

Organisations have been the subject of considerable research in the fields of management and sociology. Most research aims to categorise organisations, understand their structures and suggest ways to optimise their efficiency. Repeating many of these ideas here would be unproductive and may turn the reader into a stone gargoyle. One thing is clear though, in the commercial sector, innovation is paramount. Worryingly, in the US, the rate of patent filing has declined for the first time since records began[88]. Innovation – or the productive use of invention, is the building block of our future. Whether we are solving a major problem such as the source of sustainable energy, a cure for cancer, or devising new forms of entertainment, it plays a central role in bringing the best ideas to the fore. However the fountain of innovation is fed by a deep well of creativity. Keeping that well in good order and maintaining the fountain is a vital activity that all organisations need to address; allowing it to atrophy makes disaster a certainty. This is open knowledge and accepted as part of good business practice, however many of our organisations were designed for a different age, an age that consumed the water from the well but did not replace it. The way we manage - through rules, hierarchies and formal relationships is becoming outdated and obsolete.

In the modern world of commerce there is a new pressure driving the convergence of business and creativity. Today's talented employees are unlikely to respond to a managerial model based on the principles of the factory. In a world where automation can take care of most of the simple things including a good deal of management, something new is required. However our track record of devising effective methods of coping with our changing world isn't great, industrial dispute and strike action have been a hallmark of the 19th and 20th centuries and it seems we are condemned to operate sub-optimal systems when it comes to sorting out who does what, and how they are rewarded.

Business models

There are a million and one strategic models to help a business become more creative. Consultants such as Price Waterhouse Coopers[89], McKinseys[90] or many smaller local business consultants, including university business schools, can provide an injection of ideas and systems to help. Most of these ideas will start with staff, aiming to engender a new sense of motivation, and encouraging a new perspective. Eventually idea funnels, decision gates, and alignment tools will be applied. There is even more help available if innovation management is a priority, including scoring mechanisms and audits. These systems are invariably based on measurable performance indicators, they sit well within existing management and financial structures but do not address the emotional and intuitive changes needed to make creativity happen.

The terms creativity and innovation are often confused, but it is true that in the formal business world most executives are more comfortable with the notion of innovation than creativity. Creativity is often dismissed as an 'arts' issue. However innovation is an impossible outcome unless it is linked to creativity.

As an alternative to hiring consultants to devise a system of creativity management, it may be useful to look at what others do and copy them - not a bad idea particularly if the business is in the same sector. A company offering a creative job environment is likely to be doing pretty well, staff turnover is likely to be low, and profits high. This makes sense, as business is about offering something everyone wants at a price they can pay. How do you find out what everyone wants? by combining market research with creative problem solving. Once the market is understood it is time to develop a suitable unique product. Get creative, not once but all the time because after the launch the competition will be trying to catch up. This is how Apple Corporation[91] became one of the largest companies in the world (at the time of writing) and how Microsoft became the fastest growing company ever. There is a good reason why we migrate to from version to new improved version of MS Windows[92] every few months. However be warned - all companies have a culture, a bit like countries or towns and regions. Sometimes borrowing ideas works well, sometimes it doesn't.

So we're not going to address all the models that can be used or explain exactly how successful companies manage creativity. There is a ton of literature out there about that - easily found through the internet.

The ideas we are going to talk about are based around changing what any company can do to introduce and manage creativity, but how it pans out will depend on the culture and the people. If the company is working on new products, has a system for managing creativity and everyone is happy, great. If not these ideas might help to get to a new place with a sustainable future. This is urgent work - the internet is amazing at connecting us together in new ways, but it is also the fastest way to lose a competitive edge and those valuable staff. Today's new products and skills can be superseded faster than ever and in surprising ways - for example just think what 3D printing might do to the architecture business?

(By the way, forget sending a memo round telling everyone that from now on creativity is a priority – that won't work)

Making space in a formal environment: A 'Tardis' approach

As we've seen, a creative environment is different from a formal business environment. Most of us now work in the latter, but we know in our hearts that if we worked in a creative job we would be happier. Many of those who work in a business environment give up their leisure time to do something creative they love; the aim here is to get something of that lifestyle into the formality of modern business. The stereotypical claim that 'most people hang their brains up at the door of the office in the morning, and pick them up on the way out in the evening' is sadly accurate; these employees need a reason to hold on to their creative minds.

As a starting point we're going to 'visit' an imaginary but typical large television production company (the authors acknowledge that many programmes are now produced by small independents, but they are usually selling their product to the bigger companies).

From an operational point of view television production is managed like a huge air traffic control exercise. For the big players it is a 24/7 365 operation. Planning runs at least two years ahead of broadcast, and broadcast slots are determined with more and more accuracy as the launch day approaches. Imagine having to fill ten TV channels with content every day of the week - the schedules, the programmes, the production timescales. It involves every type of skill: actors, scriptwriters, technical production crews, accountants, IT specialists, administrators, researchers, sales specialists, external collaborators and management. Multiple productions take place often overlapping. Scale and budgets vary enormously – think about the production of a series like the UK's *Downton Abbey*[93], or the acclaimed US series *Breaking Bad*[94]. How big a team would you need to cover events like the Olympics? The teams have to work together despite their differing backgrounds. Is there ever any friction? You bet. Is there creativity? there has to be.

So what we need is something of this world in our world. We want the flexibility (or as it's now rebadged – agility) we want our people to work together on one project, then when it's complete break apart and do it all again with different people without making a fuss. We want them to come up with new ideas, to test these ideas against what seems plausible, and to create a future full of our new products (programmes). We want to make these products, sell them and grow the business.

The process we are proposing borrows from game theory. The intention is to develop a way of working that allows for creativity, but becomes systemic – that is it eventually has a business process around it that can be managed.

For the purpose of this exercise we will call this approach 'Tardis'[95] borrowing a BBC *Doctor Who*[96] concept of something larger than it appears, disguised to fit in with its environment, that also can do stuff that is not immediately obvious, like time travel and predicting the future.

'Tardis' then is a game that involves setting up a product team, whose aim is to deliver an imaginary product. Pretty simple so far. In business there are usually a couple of things that need to be on everyone's radar, such as what's going on in technology land, and what's happening in the market? But let's leave it there. It is easy to swamp the boat with information that may make paddling difficult. We will call the group who seek out this information the 'radar gang'. The 'Tardis' itself is a physical space. In this space are relevant tools, which include access to any online information sources, but also relaxation tools and toys such as stress balls. In this space, rules are hung up at the door.

Generation

The team are multi disciplinary that is someone from every

department – if that's possible. A script is written in which the team are given market information, and asked to come up with possible ideas for products. The script also contains 'curve balls' – for example improbable financial constraints, competitor behaviours or unexpected business plans. Outsiders are included, whose role is to listen first and contribute later. They should be from somewhere different, without detailed knowledge of the business but with business knowledge. The team leaders are those who orchestrate the production of the product – the director and the producer who need this team to come up with ideas.

In session 1 (scene 1), there will be a discussion, stimulated by the information and aims. Diverse thinking techniques can be used to come up with ideas and gathered until no more emerge. There will be ownership issues, as individuals and groups can become emotionally attached to their ideas. This is a break point for observation and reflection as the game changes, and is now about how to improve on the ideas collection scene. Did we get enough participation (drama) and were our people fully engaged?

Sorting

The next scene is a test with the aim of checking the ideas and sifting those that seem promising. There are number of ways to do this but none is prescribed; instead the team are asked to find ways to test their ideas, impartially and fairly.

At each scene best practice must be captured.

Within the 'Tardis' space, tools and toys can be employed at will. The information tools are there to allow teams to try out new avenues of thought and employ any methods they deem reasonable. The space is intended to be open and relaxing – conducive to creativity. In this environment deadlines are irrelevant, engagement is critical.

As decisions are made – or not made – the director and producer will codify how the process is working, as a set of best practice results, which become the assets of the game. These will eventually be used to set up a permanent bespoke facility within the business.

So what are we looking for? Divergent thinking, problem identification, confidence, engagement and risk taking will be in evidence. The objective is to encourage and develop these skills as far as possible for both individuals and groups. What seems to work and what does not need to be openly discussed. It may be that personalities, prejudices or fear of failure may militate against these objectives: these need to be overcome as fast as possible.

Reflecting

Have you ever watched a group of people talking together? If one begins to swing their leg (a common occurrence) soon others will join in without thinking. This is reflection, trying to be cooperative and collaborative. Don't worry, it's natural. The best way to begin the journey towards what we could call *creative solution management* is to be natural. Creativity works best when it is unconstrained.

Culture

Every business will have a culture. That culture will determine how people interact, as it does in wider society. The *creative solution management* that is appropriate to an organisation may be very different from other organisations. Airline pilots need to be very logical, precise and reliable, so their training emphasises that. Don't expect their culture to be the same as technicians at Sony or floor managers at a supermarket chain such as Tesco.

Be aware that historical culture is often determined by founding owners and leaders. For example, why does the loudspeaker manufacturer *Bose* carry out so much research? Because that's the way Dr Bose, the founder, wanted it to be. It was like that at the start and it's still like that today[97].

Don't expect too much too early. It can take time to find a new way of working after years of Taylorist work processes. The results will come, and the staff will find a new *enjoyment* in their work, and that's a word we want to encourage.

Celebration

A product or set of products will emerge, and at this point the game shifts into presentation mode. Players are challenged to put together their thoughts and favoured ideas into a convincing display, either a presentation or something appropriate such as a demonstration of a model or a video. We are looking for the team to develop confidence about their problem solving abilities, new skills, a widened capacity to learn from others, enhanced collaboration and a future focus. A tall order if this is the first time through the game, so as with all games don't expect to become a grand master in one session.

The teams' colleagues are invited to be the audience in these sessions and to provide feedback.

Refinement: what worked and what did not

After the party questions about the future need to be raised. How far have we come? Are we moving towards our goal? Have we reached a better place and have there been unexpected events? What has diverted us – maybe we are still behaving as if we are sitting at a desk?

Gathering this information will help to set the stage for further episodes of the game. Each episode will become more effective, and eventually a formula will emerge. At this point you have a successful production – one that can be repeated with other players.

For future episodes a similar product development challenge can be issued, but now the process is known. This process is one that fits with your organisation's culture and history as well as being owned and developed by the people who work there now. Of course new blood may be needed to maintain the energy, but that is all part of moving on into new territory.

Assassins

Any new idea needs to be more than just a good idea, it has to be supported and nurtured. It is very easy to dismiss change, and gather supporters to resist it, so be warned. Do some homework – find out who is for and who is against, and act accordingly.

Mop up

So game over – for now. The game can be played several times, until a satisfactory process is found. At that point the '*Tardis*' becomes part of the process. It is used as part of product development and planning, and everyone is involved.

Look around and learn

Understandably some may still want to know what the major players are up to. Here are a couple of examples from two of the front runners. They aren't using a game approach but they have thought about the need to maintain creativity, and they're doing very well.

Here's what Google have to say[98].

'At Google, we think business guru Peter Drucker understood well how to manage the new breed of knowledge workers. After all, Drucker invented the term in 1959[99]. He says knowledge workers believe they are paid to be effective, not to work 9 to 5, and that smart businesses will "strip away everything that gets in their knowledge workers' way." Those that succeed will attract the best performers, securing the single biggest factor for competitive advantage in the next 25 years'.

The following list contains a few admin rules from Google, which we do not fully explore as almost everyone has some version of these, but the more unusual items are worth expanding on.

1. Hire by committee.

2. Cater to their (employees) every need.

3. Pack them in (hot-desking).

4. Make coordination easy (between teams).

5. Eat your own dog food: 'Google workers use the company's tools intensively. The most obvious tool is the Web, with an internal Web page for virtually every project and every task. The pages are all indexed and available to project participants on an as-needed basis. They also make extensive use of other information-management tools, some of which are eventually rolled out as products. For example, one of the reasons for Gmail's success is that it was beta tested within the company for many months. The use of e-mail is critical within the organization, so Gmail had to be tuned to satisfy the needs of some of our most demanding customers – their own knowledge workers'.

6. Encourage creativity: 'Google engineers can spend up to 20 percent of their time on a project of their choice'. There is an approval process and some oversight, but basically creative people are allowed to be creative.

7. Strive to reach consensus: Modern corporate mythology has the unique decision maker as hero'. Google adhere to the view that the 'many are smarter than the few,' and solicit a broad base of views before reaching any decision. The role of the manager is that of an aggregator of viewpoints, not the dictator of decisions.

8. Don't be evil: Much has been written about Google's slogan, but they really try to live by it, particularly in the ranks of management. Nobody throws chairs at Google, they try to create an atmosphere of tolerance and respect, not a company full of yes men.

9. Data-drive decisions (evidence based rather than hunches)

10. Communicate effectively: 'At Google, operations are not just an afterthought: they are critical to the company's success, and we want to have just as much effort and creativity in this domain as in new product development'.

Some 'take-aways' from the Google experience are 'making room' and 'stripping away anything that gets in the way'. This helps with managing creativity and innovation, and remember they employ people to be creative, they value this capability and they encourage it. They also recognise that none of this works without managing day-by-day, being rational as well as creative, both are needed. Google are a company that have closed the lobotomising gap, they recognise how contemptuous behaviour can get in the way, either aimed at creatives or at business people, so any display of 'tech arrogance' or 'business snobbery' which is tantamount to prejudice means no job at Google.

A similar message comes from Film Animation and production company Dreamworks[100]: Dan Satterthwaite, head of human resources, provided an insight into his company's culture as part of an interview with Anita Bruzzese. He states that DreamWorks actively solicits ideas and receives hundreds of creative thoughts from all workers, including accountants and solicitors[101]. The main features of their approach to creativity are outlined below.

- Even ballpark (level playing field): All employees are given training on how to pitch their ideas successfully.
- Keeping it fresh: Stirring the creative juices is critical for keeping the company competitive.
- Restlessness: Success doesn't mean laziness. We get out of bed early every day.
- Wing mirrors: Look over your shoulder, what are the competition doing? Keep good staff and stay ahead.
- Give me a creativity future: Creative skills will be a more important driver of the economy than technical skills, and they will open the door at all levels and jobs.
- Solve, then collaborate: Workers must be able to solve a problem and then articulate that solution to all.

Most or at least some of these abilities and behaviours chime well with our imaginary temple, and with the shape of our *'Tardis'* space. Like Google, DreamWorks have found their own unique way of managing creativity using it to build their company whilst linking it to everyday management. They both make money, lots of it, but at their heart is creativity.

Horizons about business and creativity

Customers are becoming more powerful. It's becoming easier to change to other products and services, so knowing how customers are thinking and behaving is becoming a game changer. Big data based on internet transaction records is a new growth business; at the heart of this is a new empathy with customers. This is highlighted as a central success strategy by consultant Dev Patnaik. In his 2009 book *Wired to Care*[102], he argues that a major flaw in contemporary business practice is a lack of empathy inside large corporations. He states that lacking any sense of empathy, people inside companies struggle to make intuitive decisions and often get fooled into believing they understand their business if they have quantitative research to rely upon. Patnaik claims that the real opportunity for companies doing business in the 21st century is to create a widely held sense of empathy for customers, pointing to Nike, Harley-Davidson, and IBM as examples of 'Open Empathy Organizations'. Such institutions, he claims, see new opportunities more quickly than competitors, adapt to change more easily, and create workplaces that offer employees a greater sense of mission in their jobs. In the 2011 book *The Empathy Factor*[103], organisational consultant Marie Miyashiro similarly argues the value of bringing empathy to the workplace, and offers non-violent communication as an effective mechanism for achieving this. It's simple, change or die. If the decisions are still locked inside the boardroom while the staff race to get home at five every evening, your company is doomed.

What governments can do: Improving infrastructure

What is infrastructure?

Infrastructure can be viewed as a giant climbing frame. We live within it, finding what we need by traversing it. Like any climbing frame it has pathways through it, and tangible stuff within it like roads, railways, airports, schools and so on but it also has policies, politics, rules and regulations. We build it, it didn't arrive from Mars; we own it and control it through a democratic or sometimes undemocratic process. Importantly, the infrastructure provides a way of developing young people for the world of work. It is vital that it prepares the next generation for the new world, develops the ability to be innovative and explore the unexplored as well as provide the ability to maintain what is still required from the old. Some of the most important components of these 'mega systems' are the education and training systems. It has been observed that of all the systems within the infrastructure, education is the one that seems to have made little or no progress since universal availability was introduced in the 19th century. It would be possible for a teacher from 1890 to time travel to a school in our time and find that they could still teach in largely the same way. This doesn't apply to any other discipline such as medicine or engineering: they would be unrecognisable. For the infrastructure to be effective the focus needs to remain on the needs of the future. If this is lost, for example by a rigid adherence to past methods and principles, the knowledge and skills required to be part of the new world will be missed, and economic and social failure is inevitable.

In 2011 the UK's innovation agency NESTA published a report entitled *'Two can Play'*[104]. This detailed the state of the video games industry in the UK, an industry that was once the world's number two and had innovative and specialist capability and capacity. The industry needs graduates with strong creativity, mathematical, technology and artistic skills, but they complain that they cannot find these people, so today the UK industry is being overtaken by Canada and Japan. The reason is heavy investment by those countries to support those industries (there is no support in the UK) and the engagement of their education institutions to produce suitably trained graduates. The report states that in 2011 there were over 1500 vacancies in the UK industry, but only 14 applicants, and only two UK institutions were capable of producing graduates with suitable skills.

Infrastructure or 'what governments are supposed to be doing' is an essential link in the chain of a sustainable future. While the rhetoric of the old ways bounces around the media and finds an easy home in the policies of governments too weak to address the future, the well-being of all is at stake.

Those who have a role in managing infrastructure need to consider if the balance of skills they are producing for this century are correct. Adherence to the principles that defined the industrial and post-industrial eras will not work. Those eras have passed, and those solutions are no longer optimal. We do not require more accountants and auditors.

Will anything change?

Put most of the money on 'no'. There are powerful interest groups that will try to kill off any shift away from logic and rationality as the mind-set we should all have. All our systems from education through to work environments, production and consumption are now geared to work within this half human world. These groups – including most western political parties - have an ideology, money and influence. There is little appetite for change or the courage to rock the boat among leaders of the world's biggest economies, short term gain and corrupt practice that maintains and supports the status quo is the economic blight of western capitalism.

Capitalism is agnostic in this battle as it's a mechanism rather than a religion. It's a set of principles that give rise to a system whereby capital (invested money) moves to the best return. If companies need to become creative and therefore their people need to become creative then under normal conditions a shift should occur, but capitalism is now corrupted. Instead of return on investment, shareholder value is king, and with it boardroom pay. Until that is undone, those with power will not give up their elevated position and their unseemly rewards. As happened in China in the 16th century, the populations must remain quiet and obedient, not disruptive and creative. Western civilisation, the engine of wealth creation for the past 500 years, has reached a breakpoint. Either it will fall victim to the fate of previous civilisations and creativity and innovation will be lost, or it will reawaken its energy through the creativity of its people once again. Only we can decide.

Some additional strategies for maintaining creativity by other authors

Inquisitive means creative

Steven Smith, professor of cognitive psychology at Texas A&M University.

- Look for the unusual
- Be inquisitive, that way you'll see things others will miss. This means asking questions and having a list of questions that you can refer to.
- 'Creative ideas often come from unusual combinations, the best solution is not going to be the thing everyone thinks of. It's going to be something unusual.'
- These unusual combinations, called remote associations,"' are related ideas that may seem unrelated at first glance. They are the essence of creative thinking.

Creative problem solving

To cultivate creativity, you want to increase your chances of stumbling on an unexpected link. Here are four strategies you can use in your everyday life that will train your mind to be more creative in business:

1. Shake up your routine.

To expand your creative horizons, surround yourself with a broad range of perspectives and experiences. A diverse workplace is helpful, but it isn't enough. Outside work, seek variety in what you eat, where you hang out, the types of art you look at, the places you travel, or the books you read.

'Diversity introduces all kinds of new stimuli,' Smith says. 'It opens you up to a number of new possibilities.' You are more likely to find an unusual solution when you have more options at your fingertips.

2. Cast a wide net for feedback.

We often discuss important ideas with the same inner circle of colleagues, but in doing that we can miss the obvious answers. 'Someone less expert may notice invisible assumptions right away,' Smith says. They may help you see a problem or idea in a new light. Find intelligent people with little knowledge of your business and talk through whatever you're working on now. You may be surprised by the solutions they help you discover.

3. Let go of rigid rules.

Like the queen in Alice in Wonderland who thinks of impossible things for half an hour each day, you want to train your mind to be more open. Practise letting your mind wander and come up with as many ideas as you can, however absurd they may seem. You can even be silly or funny. 'Humour helps loosen up your constraints,' Smith explains: Relaxing your standards while you generate ideas increases your openness and boosts creativity. 'If you think of 99 stupid, impossible ideas and one that works, then that was time well spent.'

4. Observe the world around you.

'When you get wrapped up in your own head, creative ideas can slide under your nose,' Smith says. 'The most creative people are always on the lookout for interesting things, even if they don't apply to whatever they're working on now,' he adds.

Keep a notebook or a computer folder full of interesting ideas, articles, images, or even passing thoughts. They will likely come in handy at a moment you least expect.

Overcoming creative blocks - Robert Andersen, Creative Director, Square.

'As a product designer, most of what I do is twofold: understand the problem you want to solve and approach it from as many angles as you can. After executing on a well-defined and accurately constrained problem in multiple ways, it soon becomes obvious what the true or best solution is. Creative block generally arises from a breakdown in this process.

'If you're stuck in the middle of the design, it probably means that you're not asking enough questions. Who is the audience? What do they feel? What do they desire? What will improve their life and create joy? How do other designers tackle similar problems? At the core of every successful design is a set of simply defined constraints that you measure your ideas against. It's all about determining the soul of a product before laying down the first pixel or pen stroke.

'Using constraints and understanding as a foundation, you should then execute as many variations you can within those bounds. There are limitless ways to tackle a problem both functionally and aesthetically, which is why you need to uncover a wide spectrum of possibilities to see what feels right. This is crucial to determining quality. Creating various options also means that you don't need to put pressure on yourself to form one perfect solution from the start. Explore the good and explore the bad—creative block does not exist here, because even a bad direction can move you closer to the right one.

'Accurately understand your task and explore immediately. Give yourself the space to freely fail, and that same space will give you the freedom to succeed.'

Aaron Koblin – Digital Creative Artist, Google Creative Lab

'They say an elephant never forgets. Well, you are not an elephant. Take notes, constantly. Save interesting thoughts, quotations, films, technologies...the medium doesn't matter, so long as it inspires you. When you're stumped, go to your notes like a wizard to his spell-book. Mash those thoughts together. Extend them in every direction until they meet.

'Your notebook is feeling thin? Then seek assistance and find yourself a genius. Geniuses come in many shapes and colours, and they often run in packs. If you can find one, it may lead you to others. Collaborate with geniuses. Send them your spells. Look carefully at theirs. What could you do together? Combination is creation.

'Beware of addictive medicines. Everything in moderation. This applies particularly to the Internet and your sofa. The physical world is ultimately the source of all inspiration. Which is to say, if all else fails: take a bike ride.'

Nicholas Felton – Designer, Facebook

'I rely on a few tactics to keep my creativity flowing. I try to alternate the tenor of my years, like crop rotations. During even-numbered years, I try to do more work and make more of a profit; during odd-numbered years, I travel more and concentrate on personal projects. In 2005 I spent five weeks travelling with an around-the-world ticket, and in 2007 I went to China, Tibet, and Nepal for three weeks. After both trips, I returned to my desk filled with thoughts and initiative to create.

'My other strategy is to keep my plate as full as possible. I tend to say yes to more than I can do, and the fear of failure keeps the work flowing.

'When I'm really at a loss—when it feels like my designs are simply circling the drain—I will leave the office. There's no point in trying to blindly bump into a solution, so whether it's sketching in the park or reading a book, I avoid trying to use brute force…it's kind of like trying to get rid of the hiccups.'

Part 4: Chapter 14: A walk on the wilder side

Holly came from Miami F.L.A.
Hitch-hiked her way across the U.S.A.
Plucked her eyebrows on the way
Shaved her legs and then he was a she
She said, hey babe, take a walk on the wild side,
Said, hey honey, take a walk on the wild side

- Lewes Allen Reed, Lou Reed[105]

Many scientists think that philosophy has no place, so for me it's a sad time because the role of reflection, contemplation, meditation, self inquiry, insight, intuition, imagination, creativity, free will, is in a way not given any importance, which is the domain of philosophers.

- Deepak Chopra[106]

Our intention in this book has been to describe the valueless and dangerous chasm our contemporary culture has constructed between our creative and rational mind. Without taking a body count the fallout is most certainly directed at a decline in creativity particularly as we age. It happens rapidly once we enter formal education and is habitualised once we take up a career. In the worst case it can lead to illness and depression, physical and economic well-being can be crushed. How we think and act determines our experiences of life, and how our thoughts emerge and what we do with them is a fascinating and complex subject. There are many models that attempt to explain this engine of ideas and how we use it; these are predominantly based in science, philosophy and religion. Here we explore the tricky terrain in these areas of expertise, our aim in this chapter is to figure out what's going on when we are thinking creatively whilst also calling on our rational skills and then explain why it can keep us healthy and happy and our organisations dynamic and human.

What is creativity? An accidental random firing of neurons along pathways yet to be formed by experience or an inspiration obtained and devised by one of our many gods? It may matter when paying homage but we can still value 'our' creativity whatever its derivation. In other words some part of 'it' belongs to us, we are responsible for it, it's ours, we can put our name to it. It's a reflection of who we are and what makes us tick. Being proud of our creative achievement is a good thing to do; it helps us to build our self-esteem and self-confidence. The world is only too happy to have new useful ideas and usually embraces them providing us with status, reward and love. There would be no art galleries, jet engines, wine or Levis without this appetite. Anyone disagree? In contrast the opposite approach rewards 'me too' behaviour, simply be like someone else, the more like them we are, the more rewards we are offered – think of the worship of 'celebrities' and the increasing popularity of plastic surgery to help us to conform to a standardised look. Of course no one can be someone else, although many may aspire to just this. If this were our ambition a life of disappointment lies ahead, with a constant need to update and follow. Expectations would be out of kilter with our reality as the model life we think we should have never materialises, and if that's not a recipe for mental illness what is?

Creativity has a key role in maintaining our sanity. Who we are is defined by our creativity rather than what or who we mimic or who we work for. It's part of our ID buried in our unique DNA. When we act creatively we are acting as our core being, and when we mimic we are simply following another's direction. Our core being is made up of our early psychological experiences, which build our unique blend of emotions, behaviours and thoughts. Creativity is a living dynamic energy that reflects who we are; exercising it everyday is just as important as learning to read add numbers together or take enjoyable exercise. It uses mental, emotional and physical energy and it enriches our spirit and is open ended: there are infinite creative possibilities. Conversely, rationality is closed: there are a finite number of possibilities. Moving between creativity and rationality allows us to explore and choose. The rules of any science, or laws as they are sometime known, are questionable not irrefutable; we may believe something without any evidence or justification or we may believe something with lots of evidence to back it up. Beliefs are what we think is true at any one time, we can approach life holding our beliefs lightly, ready to accept new knowledge and change, or we can hold them tightly, refusing to believe that anything else is possible. Our open-minded creativity keeps us refreshed and curious.

Enjoying being us

Knowing ourselves means we can appreciate and enjoy ourselves, or put another way, how can we enjoy ourselves when we don't know ourselves? If our unique creativeness defines who we are then part of getting to know ourselves is about appreciating our creativity. Ideally our thoughts would be produced by our core self, they would be about making sure we get what we want. Without this mechanism thoughts can emerge that are free to do as they please. We can get pushed around by our thoughts: thoughts that can be damaging to us and the world. These thoughts may arise from external pressures, and have no link to our core being. A bit like a dangerous virus, un-tethered thoughts wander through our minds causing havoc unless we intercept them and make a decision about their survival in our life. An un-tethered thought is one that has potential to control us, even though we may have given it life. Once we know ourselves we can stop any thought that doesn't make us feel the way we want. Constant negative thought patterns are a symptom of us having little control. Control can be built by using our imagination and comparing the thought with how we want to be. This practice builds self awareness which acts as an antidote to the most negative of thoughts.

A slap on the back

We may remember being congratulated when we were children. Our first steps, first words, a dodgy painting at school, our first essay or swimming a few yards may have led to rewards and encouragement from our adult carers and teachers. This constant affirmation that we were valued and special helped us to believe in ourselves and grow into strong adults, able to contend with a grown up world where such affirmations may be in short supply. It may also be the case that such wonderful enriching support was not forthcoming; we may have been berated, unloved and abused. As young children our early experiences determine how we see the world and how we react to it; these reactions become default pathways that become habitual. These habits help us to survive, becoming our routine way of reacting to the world, and our minds create thoughts based on these pathways. These thoughts get stronger as their intention is confirmed again and again by our experiences, taking root and becoming survivalist thoughts. Imagine what habitual reactions would be built by a loving caring experience compared to an abusing hateful environment. This is why poor parenting, arcane cultural mores about women and men, violent carers, bullying by classmates, employers, partners and anyone else in our social whirlpool can have such a long term damaging effect. These habits are hard to break, and the longer they are given to grow the harder they will be to change. Within the brain these thought patterns and reactions become neural pathways, they literally become hard wired. They become the way we survive. Our survivalist thoughts are a comfort to us, allowing us to cope with a world that seems to always react in a certain way. Our behaviour becomes contaminated by these thoughts; we may start to approach every interaction as if the outcome will be as we predict. At the same time we actively encourage the sorts of interactions that will confirm our comforting thoughts, then the circle is complete and we are caught in a cycle of events that either help us to grow or undermine us. In the most negative case we may become our own worst enemy rather than our own best friend; worse still the cycle is self-reinforcing, with each experience either building or demolishing our self worth. If we allow ourselves to be constantly diminished we begin to act as victims - blaming others, avoiding conflicts, finding reasons to stay as we are, whereas if we are being constantly reassured we act as creative beings building the life we want, dismissing valueless criticism and accepting new challenges and change in our stride.

In cases of negative reinforcement, this may lead to depression and other diseases. The cycle gathers speed as each event loads the wheel making it hard to put the brakes on, but one of the most important breakthroughs is to accept that this is happening – then we have the power to stop and change our thoughts. But until this point, those thoughts will continue to reassure us that the world really is that way, as they are locked into our survivalist memory; we are the slave while they are the master. However, our neurological brain is plastic and capable of being retrained; different positive pathways can be established and once this begins the old negative neural connections start to wither away. The journey to a more positive place can be hazardous and confusing, a part of us is feeling very nervous as we start to ignore the comforting negative thoughts and start to have challenging positive thoughts. Our survival instinct and its army of negative thoughts is being disarmed, leaving us feeling vulnerable whilst our safe negative world is being atomised. It doesn't give up easily; deception and fabrication are its hallmark strategies; evidence and determination are the antidote.

This journey can be described as a rediscovery of our true self. It leads inevitably to a point where we may be able to be genuinely creative again, almost like those early years in school. Another alternative approach is to start at the end - become creative in a safe affirming environment and get some instant positive feedback. This may build up the positive experiences that will undermine the power of negative thoughts, short circuiting the negative survivalist propaganda.

Either approach requires positive affirmations, both external and internal.

Telling ourselves that we are strong valuable people that are lovable happy and in love with the world will have a immediate effect. Being told the same thing by positive friends and mentors and that our creative endeavours are valuable will also de-power the negative thought process. The end goal is to rediscover our uniqueness and value through creativity.

Too much of a good thing

Our lives are closer to the experience of a tightrope walker crossing Niagara Falls than a stroll in the park on a Sunday afternoon. Like the tightrope walker our balance gets us from one place to another. If we fall off the rope a combination of our spiritual, mental, physical, and emotional energies will catch us and help us back on our journey. They keep us moving forward by supporting our creative and logical abilities. While creative power may fill us with new ideas and enthusiasm, it is our logical skills and knowledge that takes our ideas forward to become a valuable reality in our world. Even if we are being constantly creative negative thoughts can still undo our potential. We may have prepared ourselves to refute any non-creative logical or rational activity. In this case we react as victims every time our creative ideas come to nothing even though we may have acted to ensure failure. It is just as possible to see the world in a negative light despite spending our time being creative. We may have followed our creative pathway into adulthood and a career but still harbour negative perceptions of the world or ourselves that hold back our supporting logical actions. We may have many creative ideas but we constantly fall off the wire. In this case our creative power is undone by our repeated irrational behaviour pattern, which may take the form of demonising anything that is outside our idealized creative world. We may deliberately fail to take action that would lead to a much more successful outcome as we have a fear of that success. We may harbour beliefs about ourselves and suffer from a fear of failing in the creative sphere. Like hot air balloons our creative ideas will float away from us unless they are bound to our wrist, so we can hold them and study them, evaluate and decide how to develop them.

Get over yourself

Time is a useful but arbitrary way of measuring our lives. As we grow into adults and enjoy successes there is a risk that we feel we have reached the end of our journey, that we have completed our work. At this point we may become the very person we don't need in our life, one who can find reasons not to act rather than change, who believes everything they have learnt to date is the truth, that anything that challenges us is to be dismissed. Being aware of our thoughts allows us to intercept these atrophying ideas and remove them before they become habitual. Hence the good advice to get out of our comfort zones and try something new regularly (which may include staying in and doing nothing if this would be unusual for you!)

Forgive forget move on

Resentment - it feels bad just to read the word. Curled up in a dark corner muttering curses at those whom we blame for our predicament is an ugly place to be. We are in effect giving up our power, a power which can solve any problem. If we blame someone else we give our power to them, they become the person who can solve our problem, and we are left on the sidelines stamping our feet. We give it away so that we can bathe in an comforting bath of self pity. This comforts us. Our survival instinct and our habitual negative thoughts are keeping us safe from the possibilities that we have made any mistake and prevents us from learning or taking risks in the future.

Being and Doing

'Being rational' can be considered an oxymoron. Being is a state of inner awareness taking place in real time, it's an experience of the moment. Consider the point at which a creative idea forms. It's never a future or past experience, instead always a moment of inspiration or imagination. Being is a meditative experience, concerned with the here and now not the future or the past. Think of how a problem gets solved, there is a key moment when a solution arises, which is a result of our ability to get lost inside a problem and find our way out. It draws on our ability to experience a sense of 'being' rather than 'doing'. That moment is a moment of creativity.

On the other hand, making a decision is an example of a 'doing' activity, drawing on our rational selves. It may require creative thoughts, for example imagination about the future based on our knowledge of the past. There will be a rationale behind a decision meaning there will be some way of justifying it. In the end the decision may depend on our emotional state rather than any logic but we will usually be able to post rationalise our decision. This allows us to convince ourselves and others we were acting rationally.

To survive we need both skills. Unfortunately the balance in contemporary society is tipped heavily towards doing activities. The link between our creative and rational selves has weakened.

Multiple you

In any one day there may be many forms of 'you' in action. 'You' may be doing things that elicit emotions such as happiness, sadness, anger, embarrassment or amusement. Over a 24 hour period you could have physical feelings such as hunger, tiredness or pain and you may experience mental thoughts such as worry, elation, anticipation or regret. Each 'you' is linked to a desire, feeling or thought. All this can be going on without our intervention. It is as if we have allowed ourselves to become dependent on the external world for our direction, a bit like email overload only worse. We have become actors in someone else's production, if we step back and watch ourselves as we work through our day we bring the core that defines us into the play. Non-judgmental observation of our actions allows us to see ourselves objectively. We may ask which feelings, thoughts and desires do we want? By turning the tables on the rigid dictatorship of the external world we take control, and as a result we may decide that we want to invest in our true selves, by developing our unique creativity and connecting with our spiritual energy. As we invest we begin to get benefits; we grow stronger, and we begin to dictate how our lives are to be lived.

There are many tools that help us develop this kind of observational approach. Yoga with meditation is a longstanding practice that supports the development of our inner spirit. It is our unique spirit that sustains us and guides us and helps the many forms of 'you' throughout life. Would we wish our higher self and connection to inner peace and stillness to be in control, or to be controlled by our emotions, thoughts, and butterfly minds? No contest.

We operate best when our energies are in balance and are at their maximum, and we have a highly developed sense of control. This combined state is sometimes called self-awareness, or mindfulness. In this state we are ready to connect to the world in positive ways to achieve what we need and desire.

Wealth and strength

Weaving several strands of material together makes a strong rope. In the same way, weaving our creative and rational selves together makes us stronger and more robust. As a result we can become both materially and spiritually wealthier and more successful. We enjoy our wealth by enjoying that which brings pleasure into our lives. We are both creator and consumer of our wealth. Our contemporary economic world has features of this apparent duality:- on the one hand our success depends on the rich vein of creative thoughts that led us to develop the empires of Greece and Rome and more recently the West, built on the ideas that gave rise to the industrial revolution, on the other we act as a body of partially homogeneous consumers, as the model of consumerism relies on many people having similar desires and thoughts. The creative world of infinite possibility is seemingly challenged by a world of discreet or finite possibilities-systems have been developed that govern how we may behave and react, limiting our world of possibilities. Advertisers attempt to steer our thoughts and reactions towards their products, which may have no long term utility, and may create a new set of problems. These problems would in normal circumstances be addressed by our creative and logical capacity unhampered by past systems, science and beliefs. For example our energy requirements are just one problem among a growing set of global issues. Without our creative strand tightly woven into our lives huge risks are mounting for future generations; the disconnect between our creative and logical capability is loosening our connection with our ingenuity.

Particles the cosmos and us

If we can't touch it or see it what is it? The recent discovery of massless particles that may carry information has provided a platform that draws together the metaphysical and the physical. The Higgs Bosun or 'God' particle throws a new light on the world as understood by the scientific community. The Higgs energy exists for a very short time but causes other particles to acquire mass which implies an organising role, broadly creating something out of nothing. What does this mean for our understanding of how a thought is formed, and how creativity might be working? The weight of modern understanding is moving away from the physical world being confined to particles that we can see and touch, and more towards a more ancient understanding. Physicists, philosophers, psychologists, neuroscientists and religions are finding more areas where their ideas intersect, there is a rich and vigorous debate that is bringing these incongruent views together. Check out Deepak Chopra's elegant discussion of the metaphysical vs. the physical[107] at his web site and then take in a talk by the noted Physicist Max Tegmark[108] for an update on quantum models that explain life.

And they're off

The creation of this book, which began life as a research project, has in turn been a labour of love, a delight and a pain in the ass. We have travelled into our pasts, studied history books, delved into many different disciplines, observed our friends and colleagues, and conducted many interviews. For us, it has been a deep learning experience of the type that you don't learn from books; we have felt, lived and breathed it. It's a kind of work that has no end – there are always new connections to be made and new world events about to happen. We hope you enjoyed it.

This concludes our journey. In the appendix we share our research based findings, which we believe act to provide a springboard for further studies.

I have been impressed with the urgency of doing. Knowing is not enough; we must apply. Being willing is not enough; we must do.

- Leonardo da Vinci

Appendix: Researching the differences

'Between friends differences in taste or opinion are irritating in direct proportion to their triviality'

W. H. Auden[109]

If it turned out that those who opt for a creative life style and career were born with inherited differences, or had birth attributes that earmarked them for a creative career in some meaningful way, then perhaps we might want to cut a bit of slack towards the idea that it's all 'meant to be' and we should expect to see different values and behaviours, lifestyles, attitudes and so on. We thought so too. But before we give you the results of our own study, here are some current and not so current research results that also attempt to explore this issue.

We have already discussed the work of Mihalyi Csikszentmihalyi[110], but to recap, he interviewed 400 notable creative people from all walks of life. Among his conclusions he found that these people seem to have been kept away from the distractions that befall others, particularly in their formative years, and they were able to pursue their interests without the usual level of interruptions and misguidance. What do we mean by misguidance? Well, being advised that your areas of interest are unlikely to provide a sustainable career, or being presented with a fait accompli when looking at career options perhaps by successful family members or school officers. Also not been given the option to fail and therefore coerced into a career that is less risk, and so on. He did not conclude that these people were psychologically different, but their lives did appear to be different. For example in some cases a history of creative endeavour in the family acted as a spur to follow in those footsteps.

Academic work seemed to suggest that creatives (those who earn a living from their creativity) and those who earn a living in other ways do lead different work lives, and require different environments to succeed. In her study of environments that support creative activity Teresa Amebile[111] demonstrated how factors such as time control, evaluative constraints, motivation (rewards) and interruption rates (project management) have a negative bearing on success.

Scientific American recently ran an article by Barry Kaufman entitled 'How do artists differ from bank officers?'[112] This summarised new research published in the *Creativity Research Journal* conducted in Poland by Edward Necka and Teresa Hlawacz[113]. They tested 60 artists and bank officers, looking at their divergent thinking skills and their temperament. The results linked divergent thinking and temperament among artists, i.e high levels of divergent thinking linked to things like briskness and endurance. Bank officers were not linked up in this way. Also there was evidence of lower emotional response among artists, which is strange. The stereotype would lead to the expectation that emotional response would be higher among artists. Aren't artists supposed to be more in touch with their emotions? Overall the study seems incomplete. Artists practise divergent thinking all day long, bank officers probably don't.

Of course if inherited (nature based) differences were found in these studies then perhaps it could help to explain our frustrating experiences of trying to get these two types of highly skilled people to collaborate successfully.

Our study: mind the gap

We were motivated to explore this issue following our observations and experiences of collaborative creative projects[114]. These projects relied on harmonious motivation between freelance creative practitioners and conventional employees (in this case teachers and administrators). These projects aimed at improving the future life chances of deprived young people, and ran into some surprisingly difficult people problems. There were reports of team members declining to participate, arguments over style and content, political undermining, arrogant grand standing, refusals to carry out tasks, (particularly evaluative tasks), poor quality work, poor resource planning and unhelpful management. 'Camps' developed: some that believed in the cause and those that were sceptical. This was more akin to the sort of behaviours found during difficult change projects, where staff may be asked to re-apply for their jobs, or new systems are being introduced that may mean redundancy for the workforce. Piecing this together it seemed to suggest a wide difference in expectations with arrogant behaviour from both sides, in meetings and in social settings. We had read the reports where distressed team members were at their wits' end trying to make the project work, and we were aware of work being passed off as 'creative teaching and learning', just to tick the box, get paid and move on. The conflicting behaviours appeared to be defensive, stemming from fear, and in some cases leading to anger. This didn't mean it had any substance, or that we had discovered anything more than a managerial issue.

Our focus for the research was on the effect of placing those with different work lives in collaborative circumstances, where one party is likely to experience unfamiliar challenges, and both parties are developing novel relationships. Perhaps there were some fundamental values and beliefs, like a belief in absolute freedom, or values like a rejection of bureaucracy, that underpinned the friction. So we set out to test the proposition that there were values and beliefs that needed to be understood. The great hope was that this could lead to a much better understanding between the two groups in the future. We called the research 'Mind the Gap'.

The issue seemed to be: why would two groups of highly qualified well-meaning people aiming to improve the life chances of disadvantaged children not get along?

For the testing process we designed a questionnaire available online and in paper form. We analysed comments made in project reports that indicated areas of friction, for example 'The practitioners never turn up on time' or 'the teachers just sit by and do not contribute'. We then constructed 34 pairs of questions asking for an agree/disagree response to opposing viewpoints reflecting the areas of friction, so in our example we constructed a pair of questions with opposing viewpoints about timekeeping and participation. In short the questions were designed to highlight discrimination between values and beliefs.

Example: One area that appeared to cause dissent was the need to complete evaluations, which suggested that dealing with bureaucracy may be a distinguishing factor. So to test for sensitivity to bureaucracy respondents were asked to agree or disagree with the following statements - Q 1 - Filling out forms is a waste of time, with Q 1a - No money should be spent until plans have been agreed. The expectation would be that one group would favour Q 1 while the other would favour Q 1a. For the study the questions were randomly sorted, so the relationship between them was hidden, and of course they were re-numbered.

Three groups were identified and asked to complete the questionnaire. Those who worked as creative practitioners – group 1- earned their living primarily from creative work. Group 2 were employees who had been employed for over two years, and group 3 were employed teachers. The idea here was to see whether differences existed between the three groups, not only those we had been working with, but also to test whether those who worked outside the education sector had different views.

It was tough getting creative practitioners to complete the questionnaire. Of the three groups they complained the most, and had the largest failure rate – that is they started the questionnaire but failed to complete it. The most common complaints were about the questions – some angry that they were even being asked this sort of question. (Some used 'rich' language to vent their anger). In contrast the employed group (non teachers) seemed to enjoy the task. Some were intrigued and asked for copies of the results. Among the teaching group some found 'errors' – repeated questions (although this was deliberate) and some made corrections or suggested alternative text to the questions, to clarify their answers.

It took two months to gather sufficient responses. The final total was: Creatives 21, teachers 38, other employed 43.

In summary the results were a surprise. We had expected many paired statements to highlight fundamental differences that would help explain why the creative practitioners and the teachers were finding collaboration difficult, and how those differences may be repeated in other working environments, but out of the 68 questions only a handful indicated significant differences and those differences appeared to be related to workplace experience rather than fundamental values or beliefs. Of course the study would need to be repeated with a larger sample and more time devoted to these observations to confirm these results, but given the level of attrition we had experienced the results were unexpected.

Kiss and make up

Broadly our research suggests that the gap is a product of working cultures and experience rather than fundamental values and beliefs – i.e. under the skin we are all the same. But pandering to the stereotypes is damaging to both groups – exercising a form of prejudice – manifesting as arrogance and defensiveness.

Our findings suggested that the gap is not fundamental, or one that is impossible to overcome. The picture that emerges is that it is based around experiences – indicating a strong ingroup/outgroup structure, a consequential lack of understanding and knowledge of the external group, and fear of unknown systems and processes. These components suggest a form of prejudice predicated on constricted worldviews rather than a physiological or psychological dependence on the left or right thalamus.

Here are a list of observations that help to form a view of the type of remedies that may be applied.

There are no fundamental attitudes or beliefs that mean collaboration between creative and conventional employments is impossible or requires life-changing interventions.

Division and conflict in terms of behaviours and attitude are more likely explained by experiences of working environments and working practice than intrinsic psychological make up. The gap is therefore more likely made up of tensions and friction based on prejudice.

Some environments lend themselves to the value set held by each group. For example thinking time is most valued by creatives, and we can understand why this may be. It is also valued by the other groups, but may not be obtainable. Someone who is spending time thinking in a pressured environment may not appear to be working very hard.

Preconceived intolerance and defensive reactions are likely to give the appearance of arrogance, which within an environment where respect is compromised may lead to considerable friction.

In these circumstances there may be enhanced reliance on first impressions, where this type of decision making takes precedence. Appearance, language and status will be given priority when determining relationships – the factors that cause so much intolerance and prejudice in other areas.

There are no fundamental reasons why creatives should find business difficult, and no reason why non-creative employees or employers cannot be creative or should find being creative impossible. This explains why both groups can claim examples of being successful at being creative and being business-like. There were some respondents who took issue with the concept that a non-creative and creative dichotomy could exist, quoting examples of 'creative non-creatives' (such as Merchant bankers Merrill Lynch) and 'successful creative' (such as The Royal Opera House, London) This reaction is itself defensive and an indication of sensitivities about the term 'creative' reinforcing the view that the gap in understanding is deep-rooted.

Time management and extrinsic time controls (such as meetings and deadlines) are not a hallmark of the creative industries. Formal settings with strict time controls are unlikely to foster creative work, and are at risk of alienating creative contributors.

There are many people working in the non-creative sector who don't understand or enjoy business, and are partly innumerate – it's not an exclusive skill deficit of the creative sector and similarly there are many in the creative sector who are very numerate and understand business – it's not an exclusive trait of the non-creative sector.

Where to now?

Changing the way we work is never easy. To get to a better place we will need to think about ourselves as well as the systems we use and the organisations we work within. We hope we've shown that it is entirely possible. It's not about giving up on anything, it is about adding a hell of a lot.

Questionnaire and results

Statements:

1. Having time to think is more important than administrative tasks such as accounting and book-keeping (P)
1a. Rigorous attention to detail will mean less work later on (E)
2. It is more effective to work in an unrestrictive an open-ended environment (P)
2a. Formal processes and rules are the best way to maintain quality and output (E)
3. Young people need space to develop their innate skills (P)
3a. Being clear and monitoring closely is the best way to manage young people (E)
4. All bureaucratic form filling is a waste of time (P)
4a. Information is needed before any money gets spent (E)
5. New initiatives provide the most satisfaction (P)
5a. Routine jobs provide an opportunity to do the best work (E)
6. Work is the most important activity in life (P)
6a. Work should be delivered on time and within budget (E)
7. Mixing work and leisure is easily accomplished (P)
7a. Work and leisure are best kept apart (E)
8. It is productive to look for new directions and opportunities at all times (P)
8a. There is a need to get the job in hand done before moving on (E)
9. Discipline is needed to ensure successful adoption of new ideas (E)
9a. Enthusiasm is all that is needed to get a new idea off the ground (P)
10. Confidence stems from wealth and knowledge (E)
10a. Being able to create provides the energy to keep going (P)
11. Tasks are best carried out one step at a time (E)
11a. An understanding of the big picture helps to get all the tasks underway at once (P)
12. Problems can only be solved in a methodical and disciplined manner (E)
12a. Freedom to think is the best way to tackle difficult problems (P)

13. Concentration stems from quiet environments and attention to detail (E)

13a. Stimulating environments help to get the job done (P)

14. Valuable lessons are learnt from random experimentation (P)

14a. Experiments can be costly and valueless unless they are controlled and managed (E)

15. Young people are primarily interested in modern digital media (E)

15a Young people need challenges and radical change to allow them to blossom (P)

16. Experts are difficult to work with (E)

16a. It is much easier to work with people who are ready to learn (P)

17. An effective reward is often just a pat on the back (E)

17a. People should be appreciated and rewarded for all the tasks they carry out (P)

18. Taking risks is the only way to gain success (P)

18a. Trying new things without knowing where they may lead is foolhardy (E)

19. Change comes naturally (P)

19a. Make sure of your ground before moving on (E)

20. The best way to get things done is to do them yourself (E)

20a. Working with others gets the job done quicker (P)

21. You can usually tell how people will respond in the first few minutes of meeting them (E)

21a. Taking time to get to know someone provides a much more accurate picture of who they are (P)

22. Most training can be learnt on the job apart from very specialized skills (P)

22a. Standards and training are the key to a highly effective workforce (E)

23. Professional people are the easiest to work with. (E)

23a. In general professional people can be aloof and remote (P)

24. New successful experiments should be adopted immediately (P)

24a. Even when something new looks promising it is best to stick with what works until it is proven (E)

25. Management must be respected (E)

25a. Staff must be given respect and freedom (P)

26. Advice can be discarded if it gets in the way of progress (E)

26a. Progress is only useful if it benefits all (P)

27. Risks should be avoided if possible (E)

27a. Taking risks is the only way to progress (P)

28. It is best to follow the well-trodden path (E)

28a. New directions offer the best hope for a better world (P)

29. Priority must be given to the core work over experiments and new ideas (E)

29a. It is more effective to work in an unrestrictive an open-ended environment (P)

30. If a situation is getting difficult it is best to take time out and cool off (P)

30a. Firm management and decisive action are the best way to deal with conflict (E)

31. It is best to allow experts to lead (E)

31a. Anyone can be a leader (P)

32. Much more can be achieved if you push harder (P)

32a. Finding the right pace avoids problems and mistakes (E)

33. More can be achieved with more people (P)

33a. A small team can achieve a lot more than a big group (E)

34. At conferences or large gatherings it is more effective to meet as many people as possible (P)

34a. It is best to prepare well and target those you want to meet (E)

35. New projects lead to raised enthusiasm as more people come on board. (P)

35a. Gradually improving the way things work creates the most eagerness (E)

36. It is best to get everyone on board no matter how sceptical they may be (P)

36a. There will always be people who need to be left behind (E)

37. Listening carefully before taking action avoids risks (E)

37a. Being clear and determined about what is needed is the only way to make progress (P)

38. There is no need to check with everyone before taking action (P)

38a. Everyone needs to be signed up before moving ahead (E)

Questions that indicated significant differences

Analysis: Statement 1: 'Having time to think is more important than administrative tasks such as accounting and book-keeping' (Mean = 3.41, Std. Dev = 0.929 (creatives and teachers support))

It was expected that group A (creative practitioners) would be most likely to agree with this statement. In fact both creative practitioners and teachers both agree most strongly here (means: 3.70 and 3.68 respectively). The fact that both creative practitioners and teachers are rating this statement quite highly may reflect a shared value of reflection or reflective practice. Both learning and creating are activities which require reflection whereas quite often there is less time for reflection in more conventional work cultures.

Statement 2a: 'Formal processes and rules are the best way to maintain quality and output' (mean = 3.43, Std. Dev = 0.931 (employees support))

As expected conventional employees rated this higher than creative practitioners (with a mean score of 3.72 with creative practitioners and employees at 3.15 and 3.24 respectively). This may be explained by the tendency of conventional workplace cultures to use more formal processes than are harnesses by creative practitioners.

Statement 4:'Form filling is a waste of time' (mean 2.57. Std. Dev = 0.853 (creatives support))

Again as expected creative practitioners were most likely to agree with this statement (with a mean score of 3.0.). The mean scores of conventional employees and teachers were 2.44 and 2.5. Following on from the comments relating to statement 2a, again conventional workplaces are often more bureaucratic than the small or micro environments in which creative practitioners operate

Statement 5:'New initiatives provide the most satisfaction' (Mean = 3.11, Std.Dev = 0.882 (creatives support))

It was anticipated and confirmed that creative practitioners would be most likely to agree with this statement (with a mean score of 3.65). Conventional employees' and teachers' scores were 3.12 and 2.82 showing that teachers were the least likely to agree. This result may be an outcome of the number of new initiatives that schools have undertaken over the last ten years with teachers often reported as suffering from 'initiative fatigue'. The fact that creative practitioners are scoring highest here must have implications for practitioners entering schools.

Statement 7a:'Work and leisure are best kept apart' (Mean = 2.72, Std.Dev = 1.05 (creatives and employees support))

It was anticipated that conventional employees would agree most strongly with this one, and indeed it created very polarised response patterns. However the results show that both creative practitioners and conventional employees agreed with this statement (means: 3.05 and 2.93 respectively) with teachers rating it at only 2.32. One possible explanation for this result might be that teachers create strong professional boundaries between their personal lives and their professional work with children.

Statement 13: 'Concentration stems from quite environments' (Mean = 3, Std.Dev = 0.906 (creatives support))

Based on anxieties of teachers to chaos being caused in the classroom by creative practitioners it was anticipated that conventional employees, especially school teachers would be most likely to agree with this. In fact creative practitioners were the most likely to agree (mean 3.40). With conventional employees and teachers most comfortable with noisy environments (means = 3.05 and 2.74 respectively).

Statement 20: 'The best way to get things done is to do them yourself' (Mean = 2.55, Std.Dev = 1.015 (creatives support))

Designed to test attitudes to independent working, as expected creative practitioners were most likely to agree with this statement with a mean score of 3.40. (People in conventional employment and teachers were at 2.26 and 2.45 respectively). Again the independent working practices of creative practitioners and their tendency to operate in solo or micro businesses may explain this result.

Statement: 23: 'Professional people are the easiest to work with' (Mean = 2.92, Std.Dev = 0.902 (creatives support))

Designed to test attitudes to professionalism, with conventional employees expressing frustration at perceived lack of professionalism from creative practitioners, it was anticipated that conventional employees would be most like to rate this statement the highest. However creative practitioners were most likely to agree with this statement with a high mean of 3.70 compared to the 2.98 from conventional workers and 2.45 from teachers. This begs the question of the meaning of professionalism that has been understood by the different groups within this question.

Statement 27: 'Risks should be avoided if possible' (Mean = 2.7, Std.Dev = 1.118 (employees support))

A broad statement relating to risk aversion based on creative practitioners expressing more relaxed attitudes to risk taking. It was conventional employees who rated this highest (mean 3.16) compared with 2.85 from creative practitioners and 2.13 from teachers. The difference between risk aversion in conventional workplace cultures contrasted with a risk taking attitude within teaching practice is the most striking aspect of this result. This is especially interesting as it comes from a public sector culture which may be argued has become more risk averse over the recent years.

The result may show a difference between what individual teachers think and what they are being asked to do.

Statement 29: 'Priority must be given to the core work over experiments and new ideas' (Mean = 2.89, Std.Dev = 0.882 (Employees and creatives support))

This statement was designed to express attitudes to play and creativity in the workplace which creative practitioners were expected to value higher than conventional employees. It was teachers who rated this the lowest with a mean of 2.53, and conventional employees that most agreed with it with a mean score of 3.16. Creative practitioners were not far behind with a mean score of 3.00. This unexpected result would appear to undermine assumptions about attitudes to experimentation in the workplace. Again it may be that teachers who are constrained by national curricular and rigid frameworks may be offering a personal view at variance to current workplace practice.

Statement 31: 'It is best to allow experts to lead' (Mean = 2.94, Std. Dev = 0.947 (creatives support))

Based on attitudes to formal roles and leadership it was expected that creative practitioners would value the link between leadership and formal expertise less than conventional employees. The results show that in fact the opposite was true with creative practitioners scoring this statement this highest (mean 3.55 compared with 2.86 from conventional employees and 2.71 from teachers). This result raises a complex set of questions around the nature of and relationship between leadership and expertise. It may be that creative practitioners are defending and valuing their own expertise highly in this response set. Teachers on the other hand appear to be separating out the roles of expert and leader. The notions of both leadership and expertise are called into question here.

Statement 31.a: 'Anyone can be a leader' (Mean = 2.55, Std.Dev = 1.153 (teachers support)).

This (along with statement 31) is the only paired question which remained in the list. It aimed to test attitudes to formal roles within organisations. Results were quite highly polarised with most either agreeing or disagreeing with the statement. Answers to this question however did not significantly negatively correlate with answers to question 31, which was designed as its correlate. This time teachers were most likely to agree with this statement (means...?) building on the results from the previous statement in which teachers do not see subject expertise as a pre-requisite to leadership roles.

Statement 34: 'At conferences or large gatherings it is more effective to meet as many people as possible' (Mean = 2.72, Std.Dev = 0.885 (creative support)).

Through informal feedback from creative practitioners it appeared that there is a tendency in creative work practice to build wider networks based on serendipity and possibility than more conventional targeted networking strategies might allow. Indeed results support this supposition with creative practitioners rating this highest (mean 3.2) with conventional employees at 2.56 and teachers at 2.66 respectively.

Bibliography

[1] Dawkins, Richard (1976). *The Selfish Gene*. New York City: Oxford University Press. ISBN 0-19-286092-5

[2] Drucker, Peter (1974*). Management: Tasks, Responsibilities, Practices*. New York: Harper & Row. ISBN 1-412-80627-5

[3] http://www.bbc.co.uk/news/health-19959565 16 October 2012

[4] hhttp://www.psmag.com/blogs/news-blog/further-evidence-links-creativity-dishonesty-49793/

[5] *Kim, Kyung Hee, Ph.D.* "Yes, There Is a Creativity Crisis!" The Creativity Post. N.p., 10 July 2012
(www.youtube.com/watch?v=clDZLfwzDok)

[6] Bruce Nussbaum, *Creative Intelligence, Harnessing The Power to Create, Connect, and Inspire*.

[7] http://www.creative-enterprise-network.com/forum/topics/why-do-people-not-value-our-work

[8] Tim Wu, The Master Switch: The Rise and Fall of Information Empires, Vintage; Reprint edition (November 2, 2010)

[9] http://en.wikipedia.org/wiki/Adam_Fortunate_Eagle

[10] Article from the *Miami News*, 23 September 1973

[11] Malcolm Gladwell, Blink, Back Bay Books, Little Brown Books, January 11, 2005

[12] Understanding Prejudice:
http://www.understandingprejudice.org/apa/english/page23.htm

[13] Allen, V. L., & Wilder, D. A. (1975). Categorization, belief similarity, and intergroup discrimination. Journal of Personality and Social Psychology, 32, 971-977.
 Allport, G. W. (1954). The nature of prejudice. Reading, MA: Addison-Wesley

[14] 'The In Crowd' Written By Billy Page, recorded in 1964 by Dobie Gray, Charger Records. Also in 1974 by Bryan Ferry and Roxy Music, Island Records

[15] Jones, E. E., Wood, G. C., & Quattrone, G. A. (1981). Perceived variability of personal characteristics in in-groups and out-groups: The role of knowledge and evaluation. Personality and Social Psychology Bulletin, 7, 523-528.

[16] Tajfel, H. (1970, November). Experiments in intergroup discrimination. Scientific American, pp. 96-102.

Tajfel, H. (1981). Human groups and social categories. Cambridge: Cambridge University Press.

Tajfel, H., & Turner, J. C. (1986). The social identity theory of intergroup behavior. In S. Worchel and W. G. Austin (Eds.), Psychology of intergroup relations (2nd ed.; pp. 7-24). Chicago, IL: Nelson-Hall Publishers

[17] Elliot Aronson, Timothy Wilson, and Robin Akert , Social Psychology (4th Edition), Prentice Hall; (June 21, 2001)

[18] Collins, R. K. L., & Skover, D. M. (1993). Commerce & Communication. *Texas Law Review, 71,* 697-746.

[19] Robert D. Putnam, Bowling Alone: The Collapse and Revival of American Community, New York: Simon & Schuster, 2000

[20] New Scientist: Genius networks: Link to a more creative social circle: The Goldilocks Network, May 26 2012.

[21] Bilton, C., Management and Creativity: from creative industries to creative management (Blackwells, 2006)

[22] http://www.demos.co.uk/about

[23] TED http://www.ted.com/pages/about

[24] http://www.guardian.co.uk/technology/2012/apr/29/internet-innovation-failure-patent-control?: Sunday *Observer* Sunday 29 April 2012

[25] PISA study by the Paris-**based** Organisation for Economic Co-operation and Development (OECD). Reported in the *Guardian*: http://www.guardian.co.uk/news/datablog/2010/dec/07/world-education-rankings-maths-science-reading (PISA is an international study that was launched by the OECD in 1997. It evaluates education systems worldwide every three years by assessing 15-year-olds' competencies in reading, mathematics and science. To date, over half a million students representing 28 million 15-year-olds in over 70 countries and economies have participated in PISA. The main PISA two-hour test assesses what students know and can do in reading, maths and science. The aggregate results per country/economy have informed national and global policy discussions since 2000. Results from the 2012 cycle of the main PISA study will be published on 3 December 2013

[26] Gary Hamel: The Future Of Management: Harvard Business Review Press; 1 edition (September 10, 2007)

[27] Lowell L. L Bryan, Claudia L. I. Joyce: Mobilizing Minds: Creating Wealth From Talent in the 21st Century Organization, McGraw-Hill Professional; First Edition 1 Jun 2007

[28] Drucker, Peter *Management: Tasks, Responsibilities, Practices.* ISBN 1-412-80627-5 Harper & Row (1974).

[29] Anderson, Chris (2006). The Long Tail: Why the Future of Business Is Selling Less of More. Hyperion. ISBN 1-4013-0237-8.

[30] Drucker, Peter (1974). Management: Tasks, Responsibilities, Practices. New York: Harper & Row. ISBN 1-412-80627-5.

[31] http://www.wipo.int/about-ip/en/

[32] Bruce Nussbaum, Creative Intelligence: Harnessing the Power to Create, Connect, and Inspire, Harper Collins, ISBN 978-0-06-208842-0

[33] The National Science Foundation report released in September 2010. Business R&D and innovation survey, (BRDIS), that showed that only 9% of public and private companies engage in either product or service innovation between 2006 and 2008. And then they did a second survey which showed it continued into 2009 and 2010

[34] Our dangerous illusion of tech progress By Garry Kasparov and Peter Thiel: London FT Comment November 8, 2012 6:28 pm. http://www.ft.com/cms/s/0/8adeca00-2996-11e2-a5ca-00144feabdc0.html#axzz2b0i5V9Px

[35] Is U.S. Economic Growth Over? Faltering Innovation Confronts the Six Headwinds" by Robert J. Gordon, NBER Working Paper 18315, August 2012

[36] Pharmaceutical Industry – Guardian article Sat 11th August 2012 – Peter Wilby.
' This industry is in crisis because they have no new products – they complain that new products R&D does not pay back – so they want longer patent protection. The truth though is that the number of new patent registrations are no different from the last 50 years, but 80-90% of the patents are for small adjustments to existing products. What is true is that these large companies spend almost nothing on R&D. They rely on universities to make breakthroughs. They do spend vast amounts on marketing, and supporting their share price. In effect they have no future unless they can control the market – by extending their patents – which what they do most of the time.'

[37] http://en.wikipedia.org/wiki/Aleksandr_Solzhenitsyn

[38] Ken Robinson, *Out Of Our Minds*, Wiley Capstone, 2001, 2011

[39] Ken Robinson, *Changing Education Paradigms*,
www.youtube.com/watch?v=zDZFcDGpL4U

[40]George Land, Beth Jarman, Breakpoint and Beyond: Mastering the Future Today

[41] Hungarian-born polymath and the Davidson Professor of Management at the
Claremont Graduate University, in Claremont, California, Csikszentmihalyi has been thinking about the meaning of happiness since being a child in wartime Europe. His research and theories concern the psychology of optimal experience, and have revolutionized areas of psychology, have been adopted in practice by national leaders as well as top members of the global executive elite, who run the world's major corporations. He is the author of several popular books about his theories, the bestselling Flow: The Psychology Of Optimal Experience; The Evolving Self: A Psychology For The Third Millennium; Creativity; Finding Flow; and Good Business: Leadership, Flow and the Making of Meaning. The Wall Street Journal has listed 'Flow' among the six books 'every well-stocked business library should have'

[42] Amabile has studied work environments that give succour to creativity. She indentifies 'algorthmic learning' as a feature of modern education, that raises barriers to creative development.

[43] NESTA, Playing The Game, 2010

[44] Fortune magazine 2013, 100 Best Employers to Work For.
http://money.cnn.com/magazines/fortune/
To pick the 100 Best Companies to Work For, Fortune partners with the Great Place to Work Institute to conduct the most extensive employee survey in corporate America; 259 firms participated in this year's survey. More than 277,000 employees at those companies responded to the survey

[45] http://en.wikipedia.org/wiki/Attention-deficit_hyperactivity_disorder

[46] http://en.wikipedia.org/wiki/Tiger_economy

[47] Richard Florida: The Rise of the creative Class' Republished 2012

[48] Forrester Research: The Creative Dividend, August 2014 -
Summary infographic
http://landing.adobe.com/en/na/products/creative-cloud/55563-creative-

dividends/EdyELWPe.html?ev=event13&faas_unique_submission_i
d={349C06FC-C9E6-0911-AE44-77659385381F}&s_cid=null
[49] Zidane: A 21st Century Portrait (2006)
"Zidane, un portrait du 21e siècle" (original title) 90 min -
Documentary | Sport - 29 September 2006 (UK)
http://www.imdb.com/title/tt0478337/
[50] Malcolm Gladwell, Outliers, Little Brown, 2008
[51] Dimbleby Lecture 2012, Sir Paul Nurse: The Wonder of Science,
BBC, Duration 1:16, http://www.bbc.co.uk/programmes/b01cx7x0,
Producer: Catherine Stirk, Director: Victoria Simpson
[52] http://en.wikipedia.org/wiki/Lunar_society
[53] Giving White Paper, Crown Copyright 2011, The Stationary
Office Ltd,
https://www.gov.uk/government/uploads/system/uploads/attachment
_data/file/78915/giving-white-paper2.pdf
[54] Robert S. Kaplan and Allen Grossman , How to Give Away Your
Money More Effectively, Harvard Business Review, November 22,
2010
[55] http://www.doctorswithoutborders.org/
[56] http://www.robinhood.org/
[57] Playing The game: Insider views on Video Game development,
www.nesta.org.uk
[58] Plan I, The case for Innovation led growth, NESTA 2012,
http://www.nesta.org.uk/library/documents/PlanIwebv3.pdf
[59] Advertising billboard campaign in Los Angeles, mounted by New
York fashion house Charivari
[60] Polhemus and Procter, Ted and Lynn (1978). Fashion and Anti-
fashion: An Anthropology of Clothing and Adornment. Thames and
Hudson. p. 12.
[61] Henry Rollins on 'Selling Out'
http://www.youtube.com/watch?v=s6zVUvmkyvA date?
[62] http://en.wikipedia.org/wiki/Muse
[63] Elizabeth Giltinian TED link here
[64] Wiki Link 'Selling Out' http://en.wikipedia.org/wiki/Selling_out
[65] Source Vettriano: The people's artist By Lawrence Pollard BBC
World Service arts correspondent - Last updated: Monday, 19 April,
2004, 11:46 GMT 12:46 UK -
http://news.bbc.co.uk/1/hi/entertainment/3639079.stm

Jones:
http://www.guardian.co.uk/artanddesign/jonathanjonesblog/2011/feb
/11/jack-vettriano-postcards-portrait-gallery
[66] Dire Straits, Brothers In Arms, Vertigo/Warner, 13 May 1985
[67] Ros Perlin, Intern Nation: How to Earn Nothing and Learn Little
in the Brave New Economy, Verso Books; Updated edition (1 May
2012)
[68] Andreas Wiseman, UK creative industries have 'soup kitchen
mentality,' says Lord Putnam, Screen Daily, July 2012:
http://www.screendaily.com/news/production/uk-creative-industries-
have-soup-kitchen-mentality-says-lord-puttnam/5044826.article
[69] http://www.bloomberg.com/news/2013-08-29/fast-food-strikes-
expand-across-u-s-to-50-cities.html
[70]

http://www.telegraph.co.uk/finance/financialcrisis/10308789/Ignora
nce-of-finances-has-cost-us-dear.html
[71] David Krueger, M.D. and John Mann. The Secret Language Of
Money, McGraw-Hill Professional Publishing, 2009
[72] Remi Harris, Easy Money: The UK Guide to funding Music
Projects, Music Tank: University of Westminster, 2013
[73] http://www.macfound.org/
[74] Cyril Northcote Parkinson, Parkinson's Law: The Pursuit of
Progress, London, John Murray, 1958
[75] National Institute for Clinical Excellence, Depression: the
treatment and management of depression in adults' London, 2009
[76] Stagnitti,M. Antidepressant Use in the US Civilian Non-
Institutionalised Population, Statistical Brief #77. 2005
[77] Tim Ferris, The Four Hour Working Week, Vermilion; 2011
Edition (6 Jan 2011)
[78] Csikszentmihalyi, M. (1990). Flow: The Psychology of Optimal
Experience. New York: Harper and Row
[79] Teresa M. Amabile, and Steven J. Kramer, Harvard Business
Review Press, 2011
[80] Istock Getty Images, Creativity Under Threat: No Time To Talk
About It. Related Link
http://www.istock.com, 2013
[81] Teresa M. Amabile, Constance N. Hadley, and Steven J. Kramer
Creativity Under the Gun
Harvard Business Review, August 2002

[82] Rooney, Paula, Microsoft's CEO: 80–20 Rule Applies To Bugs, Not Just Features, ChannelWeb, (October 3, 2002)

[83] http://www.imdb.com/title/tt0088846/

[84] Orwell, George, Nineteen Eighty-Four. A novel. London: Secker & Warburg, 1949

[85] Weber, Max , The Theory of Social and Economic Organization. Translated by A. M. Henderson & Talcott Parsons,The Free Press, 1947

[86] The Convention for the Protection of Human Rights and Fundamental Freedoms, also known as the European Convention on Human Rights (ECHR), Council Of Europe, 1950

[87] Linda Ellinor, & Glenna Gerard's book, Dialogue: Rediscover the Transforming Power of Conversation. New York: John Wiley & Sons, 1998

[88] US Patent applications reference

[89] Price Waterhouse Coopers, Consultants, http://www.pwc.co.uk/, Global Public Relations: Mike Davies, Director, Global Public Relations, Email: mike.davies@uk.pwc.com

[90] McKinseys Consultants, www.mckinsey.com,Email media_relations_inbox@mckinsey.com

[91] Apple Corporation, http://www.apple.com/about/, 1 Infinite Loop Cupertino, CA 95014, USA

[92] Microsoft Corporation, https://www.microsoft.com/en-gb/, Press and media Email: ukprteam@microsoft.com

[93] Downton Abbey, ITV TV Series, http://www.itv.com/downtonabbey

[94] Breaking Bad: http://www.imdb.com/title/tt0903747/, http://www.amc.com/shows/breaking-bad

[95] TARDIS, http://www.bbc.co.uk/programmes/p0129lz5/p0129m9d

[96] Doctor Who, http://www.bbc.co.uk/programmes/b006q2x0

[97] BOSE https://www.bose.co.uk/

[98] Google 'Lets Make Work Better', https://rework.withgoogle.com/

[99] Drucker, P. F. (1959). The Landmarks of Tomorrow New York: Harper and Row

[100] http://www.dreamworks.com/home/

[101] Employers value creative thinking: Anita Bruzzese's column (Anita Bruzzese is author of '45 Things You Do That Drive Your Boss Crazy ... and How to Avoid Them,' www.45things.com)

[102] Wired To Care, Dev Patnaik

[103] The Empathy Factor, Marie Miyashiro

[104] Two Can Play, Nesta

[105] Lyrics © SONY ATV MUSIC PUB LLC, http://www.loureed.com/inmemoriam/

[106] https://www.deepakchopra.com/
Deepak Chopra, MD is the author of more than 80 books with twenty-two New York Times bestsellers including Super Brain. He serves as the founder of The Chopra Foundation and co-founder of The Chopra Center for Wellbeing.

[107] https://www.deepakchopra.com/blog/article/4773

[108] https://www.youtube.com/watch?v=GzCvlFRISIM

[109] W.H. (Wystan Hugh) Auden (1907–1973), Anglo-American poet. "Hic et Ille," pt. 3, sct. D, The Dyer's Hand (1962)

[110] Csikszentmihalyi, M. (1996). Creativity: Flow and the Psychology of Discovery and Invention. New York: Harper Perennial.

[111] Amabile, T. M. (1996). Creativity in context: Update to the social psychology of creativity. Boulder, CO: Westview Press

[112] http://blogs.scientificamerican.com/beautiful-minds/2013/06/15/how-do-artists-differfrom-bank-officers

[113] Creativity Research Journal, Volume 25, Issue 2, 2013, Edward Nęckaa* & Teresa Hlawaczb, pages 182-188, Who has an Artistic Temperament? Relationships between Creativity and Temperament among Artists and Bank Officers Polish study? Creativity Research Journal.

[114] R. Sant, S. Bradley, M Fitzsimons, Mind The Gap, 2010, unpublished

www.ingramcontent.com/pod-product-compliance
Lightning Source LLC
Chambersburg PA
CBHW070314190526
45169CB00005B/1623